THE PO
DUCKS
AND THE
NORTHERN HEMISPHERE

T. BOYER 85

THE POCKET GUIDE TO DUCKS OF BRITAIN AND NORTHERN HEMISPHERE

JOHN GOODERS
illustrated by
TREVER BOYER

PB
PARKGATE
BOOKS

First published in 1989

This edition published in 1998 by
Parkgate Books Ltd
Kiln House
210 New Kings Road
London SW6 4NZ
Great Britain

ISBN 1 85585 579 8
9 8 7 6 5 4 3 2 1

First published by Dragon's World at £6.95

British Library Cataloguing in Publication Date:
A catalogue record for this book is available from the British Library.

Printed and bound in Italy

Contents

Introduction

For most of us, ducks are birds of the winter. There are, of course, the ducks on the pond in the park, but truly wild duck fly south for the winter from remote breeding grounds where there are few to watch them. Following traditional flyways, they stop over along the way before heading to equally traditional wintering grounds. Here, often in massed flocks, they bring a sense of the wild to the local bird-watcher. Sometimes these flocks consist of a single species, but most times there will be a mixture of birds wheeling on fast-beating wings. In these conditions it takes an experienced eye to pick out and identify even a handful of the birds as they speed overhead. Later, as they sit and loaf, or dive and feed on the marsh, water or sea, they may be equally difficult to name.

At close range the males of most species are reasonably easy to identify for most of the year. Problems arise in separating the less boldy marked females, the immatures, and males in the eclipse plumage of moult. But the very art of bird-watching is to develop the ability to put a name to a bird that is seen less than perfectly –

Structure of a Duck

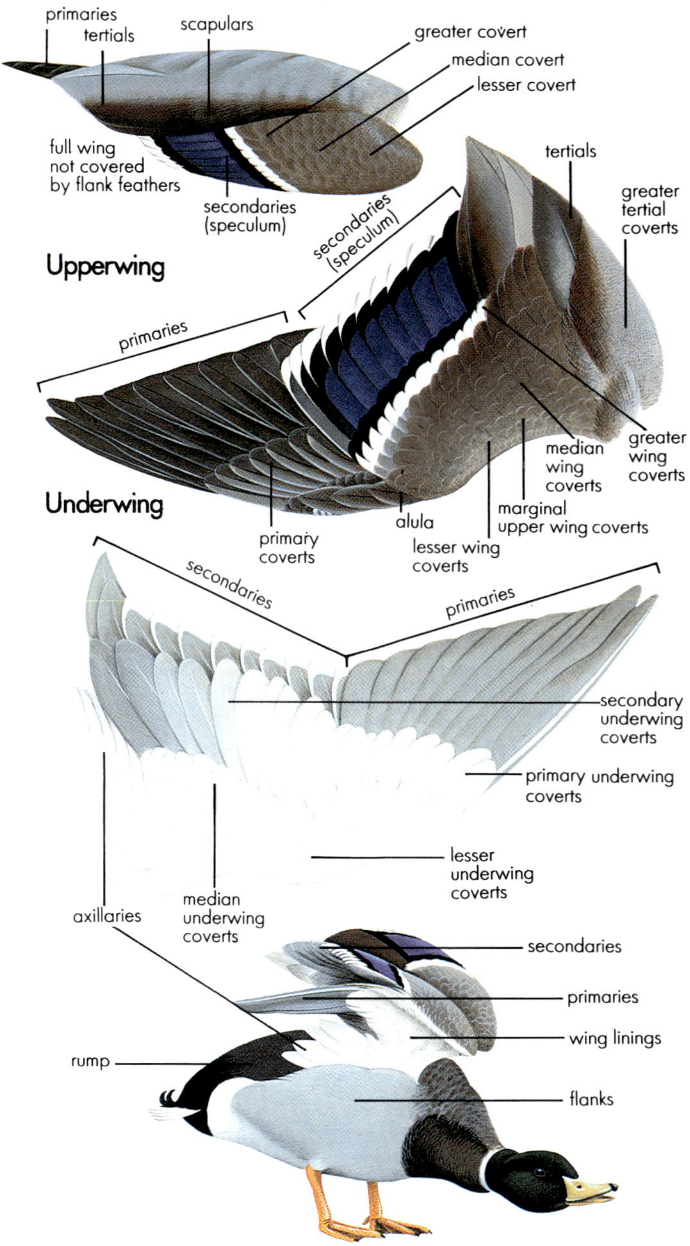
primaries
tertials
scapulars
greater covert
median covert
lesser covert
full wing
not covered
by flank feathers
secondaries
(speculum)
Upperwing
tertials
greater
tertial
coverts
secondaries
(speculum)
primaries
greater
wing
coverts
median
wing
coverts
Underwing
marginal
upper wing coverts
alula
primary
coverts
lesser wing
coverts
secondaries
primaries
secondary
underwing
coverts
primary underwing
coverts
lesser
underwing
coverts
axillaries
median
underwing
coverts
secondaries
primaries
wing linings
rump
flanks

diving duck
run along water
to take off
legs set far back
(upright stance)
surface feeder
jump out of water
on take off
legs set in middle
(horizontal stance)
diving duck:
large hind toe,
big footed
surface feeder:
narrow hind toe,
more delicate shape

perhaps for a split second, or at a great distance. All too often duck are seen at considerable distance and in poor winter light. Colours are reduced to muted shades of grey, and experience of pattern and shape takes on an extra value. Equally, and because they are so gregarious, birds often remain partially hidden, allowing only parts of their characteristic markings to be seen.

Identifying a duck as such is not too difficult. They swim buoyantly and waddle when they walk. Their long necks are extended in flight and their flight is fast and direct. Some dive from the water's surface, while others dabble or up-end to feed. On behaviour and shape alone, few other groups of birds can be even superficially confused with them. In fact, what an individual duck is doing is often a good clue to its identity. Dabbling duck seldom, if ever, dive. Diving duck hardly ever up-end. Seaduck may be found on an inland water, but only when forced there by severe weather or illness. Dabbling duck are likewise seldom seen at sea, though they may roost there for safety. Where a duck is found, and what it is doing, are both excellent clues when trying to narrow down the field. Thus, a knowledge of what to expect, where and when, becomes an invaluable aid to identification.

A few examples may help make the point more clearly. A white-headed duck on the sea is more likely to be a young Eider, which is essentially a seaduck, than a Ruddy Duck, which is a marshland bird. A tiny marshland duck seen in mid-winter is more likely to be a Green-winged Teal than the summer-visiting Garganey (in Europe) or Blue-winged Teal (in America). A vast flock of ducks grazing a damp field is more likely to consist of Wigeon than Shoveler, though both species feed happily side by side on flooded grassland.

Placing ducks into four major groups can be helpful. These are dabbling duck, diving duck, seaduck and sawbills. With a little experience most species can easily be placed in the appropriate grouping. Thereafter it is a matter of knowing what to look for in the individual species. Most of the dabbling duck have characteristic patterns of light and dark in the males, but are shaded in browns and buffs in the very similar females. Bill colour may be a useful clue in these birds, but at a distance, when colour is hard to pick out, the overall shape of the bird may be all that is available. Many of the diving duck are patterned in black and white, and even the 'red-headed' ducks look black and white at a distance. Habitat is a useful clue in, for example, separating the saltwater Scaup from the freshwater Lesser Scaup. But again a knowledge of the different shapes of diving ducks is often very important.

At sea, a distant pack of all-black duck will probably consist of scoter; but of which species? Unless they fly, or flap their wings, the bold white speculum of the Velvet Scoter remains hidden, and

Bill adaptation

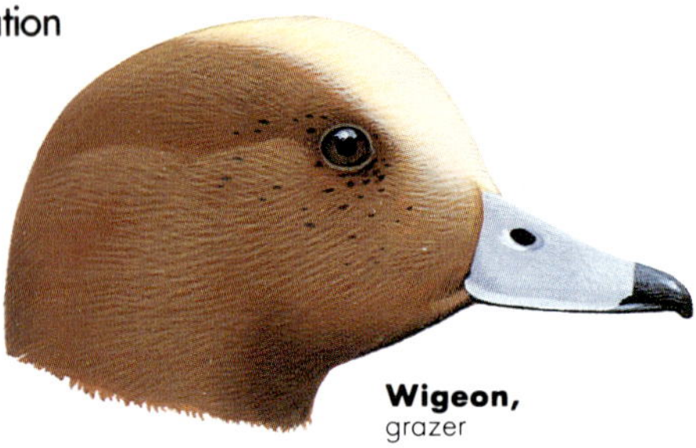

Wigeon,
grazer

Shoveler,
siever

the birds are to all intents and purposes identical. So one patiently waits and watches for a give-away flash of white. Fortunately, although the males are similarly all black, the face pattern of the females is sufficiently different to allow identification at a considerable distance. So looking for a capped appearance and a uniformly pale cheek can pick out the female Common Scoter from the twin-spotted cheek of the female Velvet. Of course, these birds frequently occur in mixed flocks, so patience may still be rewarded as one waits for a patch of white to appear in the wings of one of the males.

If features as obscure as shape are important when birds are sitting still enough to allow viewing with a telescope, what on earth can we do about identifying a fast-flying flock of them? Many groups of birds are actually easier to identify in flight than they are when at rest. The birds of prey and shearwaters are typical examples. Duck, however, are neither easier nor more difficult to identify in the air. All that happens is that the features that enable them to be picked out change, and once again it is a matter of knowing what to look for.

In flight the speculum, or inner trailing edge of the wing, is often more prominent than when the bird is at rest. This is particularly so in the surface-feeding species where the white speculum of the

Eider,
bottom feeder

Red-breasted Merganser
fish eater

Gadwall is, for example, a sharp contrast to the white-bordered dark blue speculum of the otherwise similarly-coloured Mallard. Green-winged Teal, as their name implies, have a green speculum, but so have Shoveler. The latter, however, has a pale blue inner forewing, which is also a field mark of the Blue-winged Teal and the Garganey.

Many of the diving duck have bold white bars along the upper wing and, where present, these are outstanding field marks. Indeed, their absence in some species may be as useful as their presence in others. In the case of Scaup, the white wing-bar contrasts with a black wing, whereas the contrast is much less pronounced in grey-winged birds such as the 'red-headed' ducks.

This book picks out all the points to watch out for whenever a duck is confronted. It shows all the species that can be encountered within the geographical limits of the title and illustrates each one in a variety of positions. In the last resort identification depends on the individual observer, and there is no better way of learning the art than to take this book out into the wetlands that hold duck and to check each bird against the book from every possible angle.

JOHN GOODERS

T. BOYE

Ducks of Britain and Europe

Gadwall

Anas strepera 46 – 56cm **MAP 16**

Wing (M)	261 – 282mm	**Egg colour**	Pale pink
Wing (F)	243 – 261mm	**Clutch size**	8 – 12
Weight (M)	605 – 1100g	**Incubation**	24 – 26 days
Weight (F)	470 – 1000g	**Fledging**	45 – 50 days

Identification Lacking bright colours or bold markings, the male Gadwall is most easily identified by the black-bordered white speculum which is normally visible both at rest and in flight. The rest of the male's plumage is muted brown, with grey crescent-shaped markings on breast and flanks. The bill is steel-grey, and the head is rounded, with a very steep forehead. The female is browner overall, and the sides of the bill are yellow-orange. As in the male, the clearest feature is the speculum. Gadwall swim buoyantly and fly swiftly.

Habitat Freshwater lakes and quiet marshes. Even migrants are rarely seen on estuaries. Gadwall are shy birds and often seek the shelter of aquatic vegetation.

Nest A simple cup made of grass stems, lined with down and usually well hidden amongst vegetation close to the water.

Food Mainly the soft parts of water plants, taken at the surface or just below. Gadwall up-end less frequently than most surface-feeders and are seldom seen on brackish water.
Range Two quite separate populations, in North America and Eurasia. Main strongholds are the prairie lakes of North America and the shallow lakes of the Soviet Union steppes.
Movements In North America about one million birds migrate south from the prairie breeding grounds each year to winter in the southern states and around the Gulf Coast. The winter population in Northwest Europe is about 10,000 birds, with 50,000 more in the Mediterranean and Black Sea area. Over 100,000 Gadwall winter in the western Soviet Union.

RECORD OF SIGHTINGS	
Date ______	Date ______
Place ______	Place ______
Male(s) ______ Female(s) ______	Male(s) ______ Female(s) ______
Immature ______ Eclipse ______	Immature ______ Eclipse ______
Behaviour Notes	

Green-winged Teal

Anas crecca 34 – 38cm **MAP 17**

Wing (M)	176 – 196mm	**Egg colour**	Yellowish-white
Wing (F)	166 – 185mm	**Clutch size**	8 – 11
Weight (M)	200 – 450g	**Incubation**	21 – 23 days
Weight (F)	185 – 430g	**Fledging**	25 – 30 days

Identification Green-winged Teal, known simply as Teal in Europe, are distinguished by their small size – not much bigger than town pigeons. American males are delicately marked, with a vertical white line on either side of the breast, and a chestnut head with dark green facial markings partially edged in yellow. The rear-end is black with pale yellow patches. European males have more white on the scapulars and more pronounced facial markings, but lack the white marks on the breast. Females everywhere are mottled brown with darker eye-stripes. Both sexes are identified by the green speculum when flying or wing-stretching.
Habitat Shallow lakes, pools and marshes, especially those with plenty of vegetation. Sometimes on estuaries in winter.

Adult male European Teal

Adult male Green-winged Teal

Nest A hollow in the ground, lined with grass and down, usually hidden beneath a bush or a tussock of grass.
Food Mainly seeds, filtered from the mud in shallow marshy areas. Teal feed in large groups in winter, and often burst straight up into the evening sky, wheeling about for a few minutes in perfect formation before settling to feed again.
Range The species breeds throughout the broad northern forest zone of North America, northern Europe and northern Asia, avoiding only the extreme tundra areas.
Movements Apart from a few coastal-dwelling birds, the entire breeding population, numbering many millions of birds, moves south for the winter.

RECORD OF SIGHTINGS	
Date ____________	Date ____________
Place ____________	Place ____________
Male(s) ______ Female(s) _____	Male(s) ______ Female(s) _____
Immature ____ Eclipse _______	Immature ____ Eclipse _______
Behaviour Notes	

Mallard

Anas platyrhynchos 50 – 65cm **MAP 18**

Wing (M)	275 – 306mm	**Egg colour**	Grey-green
Wing (F)	252 – 285mm	**Clutch size**	9 – 13
Weight (M)	850 – 1572g	**Incubation**	27 – 28 days
Weight (F)	750 – 1320g	**Fledging**	50 – 60 days

Identification The drake's iridescent bottle-green head, white neck-ring and brown breast make it a very distinctive bird. The body is grey above, buff below, and the rear is black with a white tail. Females are patterned in brown and buff tones, with a darker cap and eye-stripe. Both sexes have a blue speculum bordered above and below with narrow bands of black and white. Mallard are large ducks with a fast, powerful flight. On the wing, the male's breast band is a clear identifying feature.

Habitat Breeds near lakes, ponds, rivers and sheltered coasts. Very adaptable birds. Often found in city parks.

Nest A down-filled hollow on the ground, hidden among thick cover. Sometimes under rocks, in tree-holes or old nests.
Food Mallard are versatile feeders, sifting seeds and insects from the water surface, diving for water-weeds and sunken acorns, grazing on land-grasses, plant roots and seeds and shaking invertebrates from among the foliage.
Range Right across the grassland and forest zones of the Northern Hemisphere. Absent from the tundra zone.
Movements Birds of the northern US and western Europe are largely sedentary. Those of Canada and the USSR make long migrations to winter in the southern states and in a band across southern Europe, northern India and Indo-China.

RECORD OF SIGHTINGS	
Date ______	Date ______
Place ______	Place ______
Male(s) ______ Female(s) ______	Male(s) ______ Female(s) ______
Immature ______ Eclipse ______	Immature ______ Eclipse ______
Behaviour Notes	

Pintail

Anas acuta 51–66cm **MAP 19**

Wing (M)	254–282mm	**Egg colour**	Yellowish-white
Wing (F)	236–267mm	**Clutch size**	7–9
Weight (M)	680–1300g	**Incubation**	22–24 days
Weight (F)	550–1050g	**Fledging**	40–45 days

Identification Despite its lack of bright colours, the Pintail is one of the most beautiful of all ducks. The male has a rich chocolate-brown head marked with a white line running up the back of the neck from the breast. Upperparts and flanks are grey, and the long scapulars form a cascade of black, white and buff over the back. The long black central tail feathers of the male add up to 4in to the bird's overall length. The bill is a steely blue in both sexes. Females are very like those of other surface-feeding ducks, though slightly greyer overall. In flight, the male's long tail feathers are a clear identifying feature.

Habitat Very varied, including open marshy tundra, forest marshes, lakes, ponds and inland marshlands.

Nest Varies from a well-lined hollow to a bare earth scrape, always with an abundance of down.
Food Animal and plant food sifted from lake-bed mud in water up to a foot deep. (Pintail up-end for up to six seconds at a time.) The birds also feed on land, preferring seeds and tubers in winter and invertebrates in summer.
Range Pintail breed right across the Northern Hemisphere except for parts of Labrador and the High Arctic zone.
Movements Most Pintail are highly migratory. American birds winter in the southern US and northern South America; those of Eurasia travel to sub-Saharan Africa and southern Asia, but for large wintering populations around the North Sea.

RECORD OF SIGHTINGS	
Date ______	Date ______
Place ______	Place ______
Male(s) ____ Female(s) ____	Male(s) ____ Female(s) ____
Immature ____ Eclipse ____	Immature ____ Eclipse ____
Behaviour Notes	

Northern Shoveler

Anas clypeata 44 – 52cm **MAP 20**

Wing (M)	227 – 251mm	**Egg colour**	Olive-buff
Wing (F)	213 – 237mm	**Clutch size**	9 – 11
Weight (M)	475 – 1000g	**Incubation**	22 – 23 days
Weight (F)	470 – 800g	**Fledging**	40 – 45 days

Identification The most striking feature of the Shoveler is its huge spatulate bill, black in the male bird and brown in the female. The bill has well developed lamellae along the edges and these provide the Shoveler with an exceptionally efficient feeding tool. The male bird has a bottle-green head and neck, white breast and bright chestnut underparts. The back is black, and the bird's long black and white scapulars fall like a cape over the folded wing. The female is marked in buff and brown. In flight, both sexes display a pale blue inner forewing.

Habitat Inland shallow muddy lakes and marshlands, and the shallow margins of larger lakes. Occasionally seen in saline lagoons but seldom at sea.

Nest A neat cup on the ground, formed by the female twisting her body round and round and gathering in strands of grass. Sometimes in cover; sometimes in the open.
Food Small crustaceans, molluscs, insects and larvae, also seeds and plant stems, sieved from the surface water or from semi-liquid mud with a sweeping action of the bill and by prolonged up-ending.
Range Alaska, the Rockies and prairies but rarely seen in the eastern half of North America. In Eurasia the birds have a patchy distribution in western Europe but breed in a broad band across the USSR to northern China and Japan.
Movements Except for large wintering populations in western Europe and the Mediterranean, most birds undertake long migrations to the southern US, Africa, India and Indo-China.

RECORD OF SIGHTINGS	
Date ____________	Date ____________
Place ____________	Place ____________
Male(s) ______ Female(s) ______	Male(s) ______ Female(s) ______
Immature ____ Eclipse ______	Immature ____ Eclipse ______
Behaviour Notes	

Greater Scaup

Aythya marila 42–51cm **MAP 21**

Wing (M)	208–237mm	**Egg colour**	Olive-grey
Wing (F)	202–225mm	**Clutch size**	8–11
Weight (M)	744–1372g	**Incubation**	26–28 days
Weight (F)	690–1312g	**Fledging**	40–45 days

Identification The Greater Scaup, known simply as the Scaup in Europe, is the most northerly member of the genus, and its size and bulk reflect the harsh conditions in its Arctic breeding range. The male has a black head and neck, whitish flanks and a grey back, and may be confused with the Lesser Scaup in North America and with the Tufted Duck in Europe. The main distinguishing features are the larger head of the Greater, compared with the Lesser, and its more pronounced wing bar. In Europe, the male Tufted Duck is distinguished by having a black, rather than grey, back. In mixed flocks on choppy coastal waters, identification can be difficult.
Habitat Scaup breed among the tundra lakes, and by pools in the

stunted woodlands south of the tundra. Winter is spent in coastal waters, estuaries and inlets, and sometimes on flooded gravel pits. The birds often form huge rafts at favoured feeding grounds.

Nest A simple depression lined with grass and down. Where good sites are scarce, nests may be only a yard apart. Laying depends on the thaw, and may start as late as June.

Food Very varied, but molluscs (especially mussels) are a favourite food in winter.

Range Breeding range is the Arctic zone from Alaska to Hudson Bay, Iceland, and from Norway east to Kamchatka.

Movements American birds winter on the Atlantic and Pacific coasts; those of Eurasia winter in Britain and around the North Sea, around the Black Sea, and along the coasts of China and Japan.

RECORD OF SIGHTINGS	
Date ______	Date ______
Place ______	Place ______
Male(s) ______ Female(s) ______	Male(s) ______ Female(s) ______
Immature ______ Eclipse ______	Immature ______ Eclipse ______
Behaviour Notes	

Common Eider

Somateria mollissima 50–71cm **MAP 22**

Wing (M)	289–315mm	**Egg colour**	Green-grey
Wing (F)	286–312mm	**Clutch size**	4–6
Weight (M)	1384–2875g	**Incubation**	25–28 days
Weight (F)	1192–2895g	**Fledging**	65–75 days

Identification Eider are big chunky sea-duck, and outside the breeding season they are most often seen bobbing about among the waves offshore. Fortunately, the dramatic black and white plumage of the male makes identification fairly easy, and even large flocks of brown females or similarly-coloured first-year males can usually be identified by their distinctive size and shape. In flight, the Eider appears as a short-necked, heavy-bodied bird with a characteristically slow wing-beat. It often flies fast and low over the water.

Habitat Eider breed in fields, moorland and open grassy areas not far from the sea; in Scotland many breed in woods. Most of the year is spent at sea in coastal waters.

Nest A grass-lined hollow, either in the open or sheltered behind a rock outcrop or wall. The nest is filled with down, which is collected commercially for use in duvets and cold-climate clothing. Down 'farmers' empty the nest of down twice, then leave the third lining for the duck's use.

Food Molluscs and crustaceans found by diving among rocks and seaweed. Eider can dive to 65 feet but normally feed in water depths of 6 to 12 feet. Large items such as mussels and crabs are crushed in the powerful bill.

Main Eider subspecies, (left to right) *S.m. mollissima* (North Sea), *S.m. dresseri* (eastern North America), *S.m. borealis* (Arctic) and *S.m. v-nigrum* (Bering Sea).

Range Breeding range is the North American Arctic, Greenland, Iceland, northern Britain and Norway, and Siberia.
Movements Many birds make small southward movements in winter to remain in ice-free waters. Even more are year-round residents. This lack of long-range movement has created several quite distinct geographical subspecies.

RECORD OF SIGHTINGS	
Date ______	Date ______
Place ______	Place ______
Male(s) ______ Female(s) ______	Male(s) ______ Female(s) ______
Immature ______ Eclipse ______	Immature ______ Eclipse ______
Behaviour Notes	

King Eider

Somateria spectabilis 47 – 63cm **MAP 23**

Wing (M)	266 – 293mm	**Egg colour**	Pale olive
Wing (F)	256 – 276mm	**Clutch size**	4 – 5
Weight (M)	1367 – 2013g	**Incubation**	22 – 24 days
Weight (F)	1213 – 1871g	**Fledging**	?

Identification The male King Eider is quite unmistakable. Almost the entire body is black, except for a white patch on the flank. The breast and neck are pinkish-white, and the head is pale grey-blue with a black-bordered orange frontal shield and a deep red bill. Flying eider are usually seen from above, and in flight the male King Eider's black back clearly distinguishes it from the Common Eider which has a white back. Females and immature males are less easy to identify. Feathering along the ridge of the bill reaches the nostrils and creates the impression of a larger head and smaller bill than the Common Eider. There is also a pale eye-ring.

Habitat King Eider breed farther north than Common Eider, by pools and lakes in the extreme northern tundra zone.
Nest A simple hollow lined with down. Unlike Common Eider they are solitary nesters, each pair staking out a small territory.
Food Mainly shellfish, sea urchins and crabs. King Eider feed farther from shore than Common Eider, usually in water about 50 feet deep although the birds are capable of diving to over 150 feet.
Range Extreme High Arctic: circumpolar except for a gap around Iceland and Northwest Europe where the Gulf Stream makes the conditions too warm.
Movements Most birds move only as far as is necessary to remain in open water for feeding, and so winter along the edge of the pack ice. Occasional vagrants seen in Europe.

RECORD OF SIGHTINGS	
Date ________	Date ________
Place ________	Place ________
Male(s) ____ Female(s) ____	Male(s) ____ Female(s) ____
Immature ____ Eclipse ____	Immature ____ Eclipse ____
Behaviour Notes	

Steller's Eider

Polysticta stelleri 43–47cm **MAP 25**

Wing (M)	199–225mm	**Egg colour**	Yellowish
Wing (F)	203–210mm	**Clutch size**	6–7
Weight (M)	500–1000g	**Incubation**	?
Weight (F)	750–1000g	**Fledging**	?

Identification This species is so distinct from the three other eiders that it is placed in a separate genus. Most noticeable is the rounded head, steep forehead and small bill – quite unlike the wedge-shaped head-and-bill profile of the Common Eider. The shape is more like that of a dabbling duck. Males are mainly black above and buff below, with a white head ornamented with black eye patches and areas of pale green at the base of the bill and back of the head. Females are dark buff and brown, with a paler eye-ring. Both sexes have a blue and white speculum, very like that of the Mallard, which shows quite clearly in flight.

Habitat Arctic tundra in the breeding season; clear shallow Arctic coastal waters and estuaries at other times.
Nest Made of grass and lined with down; usually well hidden among tussocks of grass. The birds are solitary breeders and each pair claims a small pool as its own territory.
Food Molluscs, crustaceans, worms and fish. The birds feed in flocks and often dive in unison.
Range Breeds along the northern shores of Alaska, east to the Mackenzie River, and in Siberia west from the Bering Strait to the mouth of the Khatanga River.
Movements Generally winters in the North Pacific, from Alaska round to Kamchatka, occasionally south to Japan. Vagrants wander south to British Columbia and Britain. Flocks regularly winter and moult in northern Norway, and at times have also bred there.

RECORD OF SIGHTINGS	
Date ______	Date ______
Place ______	Place ______
Male(s) ______ Female(s) ______	Male(s) ______ Female(s) ______
Immature ______ Eclipse ______	Immature ______ Eclipse ______
Behaviour Notes	

Harlequin Duck

Histrionicus histrionicus 38 – 45cm **MAP 26**

Wing (M)	197 – 214mm	**Egg colour**	Cream
Wing (F)	194 – 201mm	**Clutch size**	5 – 7
Weight (M)	582 – 750g	**Incubation**	27 – 29 days
Weight (F)	520 – 562g	**Fledging**	60 – 70 days

Identification The aptly-named male Harlequin is dark blue, with chestnut flanks, a chestnut stripe above the eye, and bold black and white markings on the head, breast and inner wing. The female is dark brown above and pale below, with light banding across the breast. The female also has three pale patches on either side of the face, which can lead to confusion with the female Velvet Scoter or Surf Scoter. Identification is, however, helped by the neat round head and the lack of any swelling at the base of the bill. Female Harlequin are also uniformly brown in flight while the female Velvet Scoter has white in the wing.

Habitat In the breeding season Harlequin are birds of fast-flowing rivers – the northern counterparts of the South American torrent ducks. They are superb swimmers and divers, and can burst from the wildest waters directly into flight.

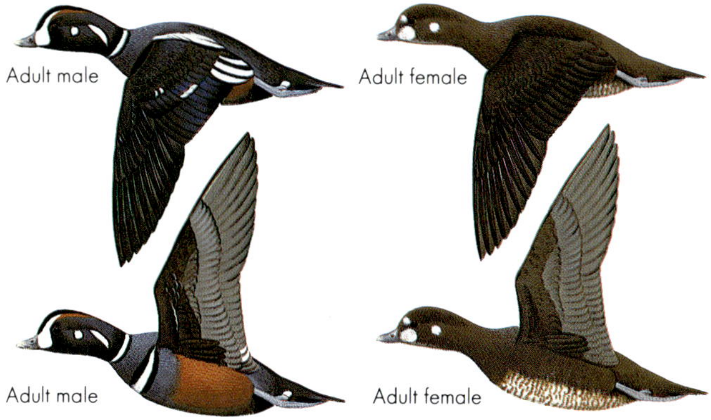

Nest A hollow lined with grass and down, usually well hidden in thick riverside vegetation.
Food Mainly small aquatic animals and insect larvae, taken when diving among rocks and gravel banks. In winter the birds feed in coastal waters on molluscs and crustaceans.
Range Two main populations; one in western and extreme eastern North America, and the other in eastern Siberia. The only European breeding site is in Iceland.
Movements In winter the birds move to the nearest ice-free coast, which for the most northerly breeders can mean quite long migrations. Wintering birds are found as far south as California, New York and southern Japan.

RECORD OF SIGHTINGS	
Date ______	Date ______
Place ______	Place ______
Male(s) ______ Female(s) ______	Male(s) ______ Female(s) ______
Immature ______ Eclipse ______	Immature ______ Eclipse ______
Behaviour Notes	

Oldsquaw or Long-tailed Duck

Clangula hyemalis 40–47cm **MAP 27**

Wing (M)	205–241mm	**Egg colour**	Olive-buff
Wing (F)	192–220mm	**Clutch size**	6–9
Weight (M)	616–955g	**Incubation**	24–29 days
Weight (F)	510–879g	**Fledging**	35–40 days

Identification The Oldsquaw, more familiar to European birdwatchers as the Long-tailed Duck, is unusual in having quite distinctive summer and winter plumages and also quite different plumages during the eclipse (moult) phase and in the first year. Apart from their attractive proportions and neat rounded heads, the birds are characterized by their small bills, short necks and pointed tails. The male is very distinctive, having long tail feathers in both summer and winter which add up to 5in to the bird's overall length. An unusually patchy head pattern is typical of all plumages.

Habitat The birds breed among the pools and lakes of the tundra zone and winter at sea, often far from land.

Nest A simple depression lined with grass and down, either in cover or in the open. On predator-free islands nesting density may be high, and the ducks often nest among colonies of other birds such as Eiders and terns.

Food Molluscs, crustaceans, insect larvae and fish eggs. Cockles form a major part of the winter diet.

Range Up to 15 million birds (5 million in the western USSR) are distributed right across the northern tundra zone during the summer breeding season.

Movements Outside the breeding season the ducks are rarely seen on land. They venture inland only in small numbers, and then often only as a result of storms or oil spills. Birds returning to the breeding grounds in spring gather in large flocks offshore, waiting for the onset of the thaw.

RECORD OF SIGHTINGS	
Date ______	Date ______
Place ______	Place ______
Male(s) ______ Female(s) ______	Male(s) ______ Female(s) ______
Immature ______ Eclipse ______	Immature ______ Eclipse ______
Behaviour Notes	

Common Scoter

Melanitta nigra 44 – 54cm **MAP 28**

Wing (M)	217 – 247mm	**Egg colour**	Creamy buff
Wing (F)	206 – 239mm	**Clutch size**	6 – 8
Weight (M)	642 – 1450g	**Incubation**	30 – 31 days
Weight (F)	600 – 1268g	**Fledging**	45 – 50 days

Identification Not surprisingly, the Common Scoter is also called the Black Scoter for the male bird is all black with the exception of the bright orange-yellow patch at the base of the bill. In the American subspecies (*M.n.americana*) the orange patch covers most of the bill. In the Eurasian birds (*M.n.nigra*) it is smaller, and the bill also has a prominent black swelling at the base. Females are dark brown, with paler plumage at the sides of the head and neck. The birds are usually seen as dark shapes bobbing buoyantly amongst the waves offshore with tails characteristically raised high, or as chunky black birds flying swiftly over the water in long lines or tightly-knit bunches.

Habitat Common Scoters breed mainly among the lakes and pools of the Arctic tundra, but also breed regularly in the north of Scotland. The birds winter at sea in coastal waters.

Nest A well-concealed hollow in the grass, shaped by the female and lined with soft grass and down.

Food Mainly molluscs taken in dives lasting up to 50 seconds. Wintering birds are often seen in flight in the morning and evening, passing between feeding grounds near the shore and resting areas farther out to sea.

M.n.americana

Range *M.n.americana* breeds in Siberia east from the Lena River and then in North America in Alaska, Hudson Bay and Newfoundland. *M.n.nigra* is found west of the Lena River as far as Iceland, including northern Britain.

Movements In winter, Scoter migrate to coastal waters. In the US they move as far south as California and South Carolina. North European birds are found from Norway and the North Sea area south virtually to the Equator, while in the east Siberian birds are common off the coasts of Japan and China. Numbers are difficult to determine but up to a million birds pass along the German North Sea coast in late summer and half as many again pass through Finland in the spring.

RECORD OF SIGHTINGS	
Date ______	Date ______
Place ______	Place ______
Male(s) ____ Female(s) ____	Male(s) ____ Female(s) ____
Immature ____ Eclipse ____	Immature ____ Eclipse ____
Behaviour Notes	

Velvet Scoter

Melanitta fusca 51–58cm **MAP 29**

Wing (M)	260–286mm	**Egg colour**	Cream
Wing (F)	232–271mm	**Clutch size**	7–9
Weight (M)	1173–2104g	**Incubation**	27–28 days
Weight (F)	1140–1895g	**Fledging**	50–55 days

Identification The male Velvet Scoter is an all-black bird very like its close relative the Common Scoter. Identifying features are a slightly stockier build, a comma-shaped white patch below and behind the eye, and a larger bill with a greater area of orange. The base of the bill is swollen but does not form the distinctive knob seen in Common Scoter. The clearest difference separating both the males and the females of the two species is the white speculum on the Velvet's inner wing. This shows clearly in flight and can be observed when the ducks are on the water as they frequently rise up and flap or stretch their wings. Females are darker brown than female Common Scoter, and lack the pale face.
Habitat Breeds among lakes and pools in tundra, forests and valleys across much of the Northern Hemisphere. Accepts a much wider variety of habitats than the Common Scoter.

American subspecies *M.f.deglandi*

Nest A hollow lined with vegetation and down, usually near water. Nests may be only a few yards apart, though the birds are not colonial. Velvet Scoter will also use nest-boxes.
Food Summer food consists largely of insect larvae: winter diet is mainly of molluscs – especially the dog-whelks, cockles and mussels common in inshore and brackish waters.
Range Almost circumpolar but missing from eastern North America, Greenland and Iceland. Velvet Scoter overlap with Common Scoter over much of their range but extend farther.
Movements American birds winter as far south as Baja California and South Carolina: Eurasian birds congregate around the North Sea, and in the east along the shores of Japan, Manchuria and southern Kamchatka.

RECORD OF SIGHTINGS	
Date ____________	Date ____________
Place ____________	Place ____________
Male(s) ______ Female(s) ______	Male(s) ______ Female(s) ______
Immature _____ Eclipse _______	Immature _____ Eclipse _______
Behaviour Notes	

Common Goldeneye

Bucephala clangula 42–50cm **MAP 30**

Wing (M)	202–231mm	**Egg colour**	Blue-green
Wing (F)	186–207mm	**Clutch size**	8–11
Weight (M)	750–1245g	**Incubation**	29–30 days
Weight (F)	500–882g	**Fledging**	57–66 days

Identification The drake Goldeneye is a boldly-patterned black and white bird with a strong iridescent green wash to the head. In addition to the bright golden eye for which it is named, and the large white spot at the base of the bill, it is instantly recognizable by the large triangular head. The female has a brown head and buff-grey body, a pale eye and a yellow mark at the tip of the bill. In flight both sexes show a white inner half to the upper wing, marked by a single black line.

Habitat Goldeneye breed among lakes and ponds in mature forests. The birds winter on large freshwater lakes and in sheltered bays and estuaries along the sea coast.

Nest A tree-hole, preferably with a top opening and no more than

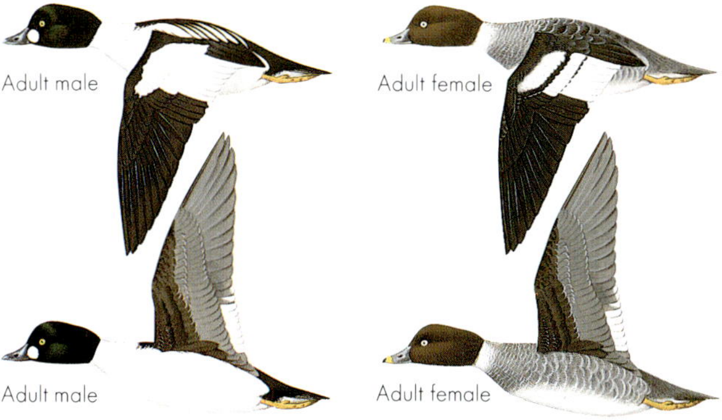

three feet deep. The same hole may be used by more than one female (occasionally by females of different species).

Food Very varied, including molluscs in winter, seeds in autumn and insect larvae in summer. The birds feed in small groups, diving repeatedly to depths of about ten feet.

Range In North America from Alaska to Newfoundland, from the northern tree-line south to the US border. In Eurasia from northern Britain and Scandinavia east to Japan.

Movements At the end of the breeding season, Goldeneye congregate in huge flocks at their moulting grounds. More than 100,000 winter in Denmark alone. American birds winter along the east and west coasts, and along the Mississippi valley to the Great Lakes. In Europe, the Baltic, North Sea, Black Sea and Caspian Sea are major wintering grounds.

RECORD OF SIGHTINGS	
Date ______	Date ______
Place ______	Place ______
Male(s) ____ Female(s) ____	Male(s) ____ Female(s) ____
Immature ____ Eclipse ____	Immature ____ Eclipse ____
Behaviour Notes	

Red-breasted Merganser

Mergus serrator 52–58cm **MAP 31**

Wing (M)	226–255mm	**Egg colour**	Buff
Wing (F)	208–239mm	**Clutch size**	8–10
Weight (M)	900–1350g	**Incubation**	31–32 days
Weight (F)	780–1055g	**Fledging**	60–65 days

Identification The most typical of the fish-eating ducks: slim, streamlined, designed (like the grebes) for high-speed underwater pursuit, and armed with a long, slender bill with a hooked tip and sharp marginal serrations to provide a firm grip on slippery prey. The drake's bold markings and ragged crest make it instantly recognizable. Only the drake Goosander is similar but that bird lacks both the broad breast-band and the distinctive ragged crest. Females of the two species are less easy to distinguish but the duck Red-breasted has a ragged horizontal crest like that of her mate.
Habitat Frequently seen along rivers with stony beds, and in estuaries and sea inlets. In winter the birds are more marine, occupying sheltered sea bays and estuaries.

Nest A hollow lined with grass and down, either on the ground, in cover, or in a rock crevice or tree-hole.
Food Fish. Small fish are swallowed underwater, larger ones are brought to the surface. Mergansers frequently hunt in groups, driving their prey into shallow water by swimming towards the shore in lines or arcs.
Range Completely circumpolar throughout the tundra and northern forest zones of America and Eurasia, including Greenland, Iceland and Britain as far south as Wales.
Movements American birds winter in the Great Lakes and on the east, west and Gulf coasts as far south as Mexico. The Eurasian birds winter around the North Sea, eastern Mediterranean, Caspian and Black seas, and off southern China and Japan.

RECORD OF SIGHTINGS	
Date ______	Date ______
Place ______	Place ______
Male(s) ______ Female(s) ______	Male(s) ______ Female(s) ______
Immature ______ Eclipse ______	Immature ______ Eclipse ______
Behaviour Notes	

Common Merganser

Mergus merganser 58–66cm **MAP 32**

Wing (M)	263–295mm	**Egg colour**	Cream
Wing (F)	242–270mm	**Clutch size**	8–11
Weight (M)	1264–2160g	**Incubation**	30–32 days
Weight (F)	898–1770g	**Fledging**	60–70 days

Identification The Common Merganser, known in Europe as the Goosander, is the largest and most handsome of the sawbilled fish-eating ducks. The male's head is dark bottle-green with a distinctive rounded crest. The back is black, the flanks are white, and the breast and underparts are flushed pink. The female is very similar to the female Red-breasted Merganser but is longer, with a darker chestnut head and a crest that slopes down towards the back rather than standing out horizontally. Males of the American subspecies (*M.m.americanus*) differ from the Eurasian (*M.m.merganser*) in having a narrow transverse black bar on the inner wing.
Habitat The birds breed by lakes and fast-flowing rivers in the forest zone encircling the Northern Hemisphere. They avoid the tundra but are found in the Rockies as far south as California, in the Alps and in the central Asian plateau.
Nest A down-lined hole in a tree (often a disused Black Woodpecker hole) or in a rock crevice, building or nest box.
Food Fish, especially herring at sea, and trout and young salmon in fresh waters. Also eel, grayling, roach and others.
Range Circumpolar, including Iceland and Britain (colonized in 1871). Absent only from Greenland.

American subspecies *M.m.americanus*

Movements In winter American birds migrate to the southern US. European birds gather on fresh waters surrounding the North Sea, southern Baltic and Caspian Sea, while north Asian populations winter in central Asia and in Japan and southern China.

RECORD OF SIGHTINGS	
Date ______	Date ______
Place ______	Place ______
Male(s) ______ Female(s) ______	Male(s) ______ Female(s) ______
Immature ______ Eclipse ______	Immature ______ Eclipse ______
Behaviour Notes	

Ruddy Duck

Oxyura jamaicensis 35–43cm **MAP 33**

Wing (M)	142–154mm	**Egg colour**	Creamy white
Wing (F)	135–149mm	**Clutch size**	6–10
Weight (M)	540–795g	**Incubation**	25–26 days
Weight (F)	310–650g	**Fledging**	50–55 days

Identification In summer plumage the male Ruddy Duck is a rich chestnut colour, with a long dark-brown tail that is often held erect in the manner characteristic of the 'stiff-tail' ducks. The nape and crown are dark, the face white, and the broad spatulate bill is pale blue with an orange rim. In winter this gaudy plumage is replaced with a brown plumage more like that of the female. At this time of year the male is identified by his white face. Females are a warm brown with soft barring and a distinctive dark line across the pale buff face. In flight a uniformly dark upper wing is a very useful identification feature.

Habitat Shallow marshes and pools with plenty of emergent vegetation and floating islands of reeds.
Nest A platform of reeds and other vegetation debris, often well out from the shore in water up to three feet deep. On this platform the female makes a neat cup for the eggs.
Food Roots, plant stems and seeds sifted from lake-bed mud. Crustaceans, molluscs and insect larvae are also taken when seasonally abundant.
Range The Ruddy Duck is an American species common in the western half of the US. In Britain it first bred in the wild in 1960 near the Wildfowl Trust's Slimbridge reserve in Gloucestershire, and has since spread to the Midlands.
Movements In winter American birds spread south to Mexico and the southern states and east to New York. Some of the small British population have been recorded in Belgium.

RECORD OF SIGHTINGS	
Date ______	Date ______
Place ______	Place ______
Male(s) ____ Female(s) ____	Male(s) ____ Female(s) ____
Immature ____ Eclipse ____	Immature ____ Eclipse ____
Behaviour Notes	

Egyptian Goose

Alopochen aegyptiacus 63–73cm **MAP 36**

Wing (M)	378–406mm	**Egg colour**	Creamy white
Wing (F)	352–390mm	**Clutch size**	6–12
Weight (M)	1900–2250g	**Incubation**	28–30 days
Weight (F)	1500–1800g	**Fledging**	70–75 days

Identification The Egyptian Goose is a well-built bird with long legs and an upright stance. The dominant plumage colour of the body is a pinkish brown with lighter buff underparts, and the main feature of the head plumage is a dark patch surrounding the eye. The wing coverts are pure white above and below, contrasting with the black primaries and secondaries to give a distinctive pattern in flight. The female is similar to the male though slightly smaller.
Habitat In its native Africa the Egyptian Goose is a bird of river banks and marshes, and it occurs in most habitats apart from dense forest and desert. In England it inhabits damp fields and meadows.

Nest The female lays her eggs in a tree hole, or sometimes in a large abandoned tree nest of another species. A nest of grass lined with down may also be built on the ground or in a hole in a river bank.

Food Mainly grasses and some crop plants.

Range The natural range is Africa south of the Sahara, with wintering birds appearing in southern Tunisia where the species formerly bred. The bird was introduced to England in the eighteenth century and is now established in the wild in East Anglia with a population of 400 – 500. In recent years this small population has shown little sign of increasing, perhaps because competition with other large waterfowl has kept the breeding success rate down to about two fledged young per pair, despite the large clutch size.

RECORD OF SIGHTINGS	
Date ________	Date ________
Place ________	Place ________
Male(s) ____ Female(s) ____	Male(s) ____ Female(s) ____
Immature ____ Eclipse ____	Immature ____ Eclipse ____
Behaviour Notes	

Shelduck

Tadorna tadorna 58–67cm **MAP 37**

Wing (M)	312–350mm	**Egg colour**	Creamy white
Wing (F)	284–316mm	**Clutch size**	8–11
Weight (M)	830–1500g	**Incubation**	29–31 days
Weight (F)	562–1250g	**Fledging**	45–50 days

Identification One of the most distinctive of all estuarine and shoreline birds. The basic pattern of black and white is recognizable at great distances across mud flats. At closer quarters the male's head is a dark glossy green, and the red bill has a swan-like swelling at the base. The white body plumage is broken up by black horizontal stripes along each side of the back, and by the broad chestnut band around the upper breast. The female is similar but less clearly marked. She lacks the swelling at the base of the bill, and has a white eye-ring. The birds fly with slow, goose-like wing-beats.

Habitat Estuaries and shorelines, especially mudflats. At high tide the birds roost in loose groups in nearby fields, often with European Wigeon and other shorebirds.

Adult male

Adult male

Nest The eggs are laid on a bed of down in a tree-hole, an old rabbit burrow, or a hole in a hayrick or building.
Food Mainly small animals sifted from the mud with a characteristic side-to-side sweeping action of the bill. The tiny marine snail *Hydrobia* is a major food item. On land, a few insects and seeds are also eaten.
Range Common around the shores of Northwest Europe and the lakes of Sweden. Also breeds in the Mediterranean, and in a broad band across Eurasia from the Black Sea to China.
Movement Before their young are independent most adults fly away, leaving a few 'aunts' in charge. The adults gather in huge numbers to moult: more than 100,000 regularly use the sandbanks at the mouth of the Elbe in northern Germany, and up to 4000 moult in Bridgewater Bay in southwest England.

RECORD OF SIGHTINGS	
Date ____________	Date ____________
Place ____________	Place ____________
Male(s) ______ Female(s) ______	Male(s) ______ Female(s) ______
Immature _____ Eclipse _______	Immature _____ Eclipse _______
Behaviour Notes	

Ruddy Shelduck

Tadorna ferruginea 61–67cm **MAP 38**

Wing (M)	354–383mm	**Egg colour**	White
Wing (F)	321–369mm	**Clutch size**	6–12
Weight (M)	1360–1600g	**Incubation**	28–29 days
Weight (F)	925–1500g	**Fledging**	55 days

Identification Ruddy Shelduck have warm orange-chestnut plumage, dark eyes, and black bill and legs. There is a white flash on the edge of the folded wing, which often remains hidden, and black tips to the long wings, which extend beyond the end of the tail. The features that distinguish the sexes are the narrow black neck-ring of the male bird, and the paler (often almost white) head of the female. In flight both male and female birds show a white inner forewing, jet black primaries, and black secondaries that incorporate a dark glossy green speculum.
Habitat Open ground with short grassy vegetation. Always near water of some sort – from freshwater lakes and rivers to inland seas and salt lagoons.
Nest A simple lining of down in the bottom of a hole in a tree, a sandbank, a pile of rocks or even a building.

Food Mainly grasses, grazed at night, often some distance from water. Frogs, worms and insects are also taken.
Range In Europe there are small populations in Greece, Bulgaria and Romania, but apart from a breeding population in the Atlas mountains the bulk of the population breeds in a broad region stretching across south-central Asia.
Movements In winter the huge central Asian population heads south to the Himalayan foothills and the plains of northern India and east to southern and eastern China. European birds winter in Turkey, Cyprus and the Nile delta.

RECORD OF SIGHTINGS	
Date ____________	Date ____________
Place ____________	Place ____________
Male(s) ______ Female(s) ______	Male(s) ______ Female(s) ______
Immature ____ Eclipse ______	Immature ____ Eclipse ______
Behaviour Notes	

Mandarin Duck

Aix galericulata 41–49cm **MAP 39**

Wing (M)	226–242mm	**Egg colour**	White
Wing (F)	215–234mm	**Clutch size**	9–12
Weight (M)	571–693g	**Incubation**	28–30 days
Weight (F)	428–608g	**Fledging**	40–45 days

Identification The male Mandarin can not be confused with any other duck. The plumage is a blaze of red, orange, blue, green and buff, with bold stripes of black and white. The sides of the head and neck are adorned with long plumes, and when the bird is on the ground modified tertial feathers on the inner wing stand upright to form triangular bright orange 'wing-sails', which are used to great effect in display. The female is soft brown above and white below, with a grey head marked with a white stripe behind the eye. In flight the small size and pointed tail are the best identifying features.
Habitat Small lakes in thickly wooded country. Also along woodland streams and in formal parks and gardens.
Nest A thick lining of down, wood fragments and plant stems in the bottom of a tree-hole up to 40 feet above the ground.

Food Mandarins feed mainly on land, on acorns, nuts and seeds.
Range Natural breeding range is far eastern Siberia, China and Japan, but the birds have seriously declined in numbers in recent years. Introduced to Britain as an ornamental bird in 1745. Escaped birds started to breed in the wild in the twentieth century. Now up to 400 pairs in southeast England.
Movements Far Eastern birds winter in southern Japan and China. Most British birds are sedentary, but a few migrate as far as Hungary. Two ringed birds recorded in Norway one November were recorded again in Northumberland, 500 miles away, just 24 hours later!

RECORD OF SIGHTINGS	
Date ______	Date ______
Place ______	Place ______
Male(s) ____ Female(s) ____	Male(s) ____ Female(s) ____
Immature ____ Eclipse ____	Immature ____ Eclipse ____
Behaviour Notes	

European Wigeon

Anas penelope 45–51cm **MAP 35**

Wing (M)	252–281mm	**Egg colour**	Cream
Wing (F)	242–262mm	**Clutch size**	6–12
Weight (M)	600–1090g	**Incubation**	24–25 days
Weight (F)	530–910g	**Fledging**	40–45 days

Identification The drake Wigeon is a handsome bird. The head is a rich chestnut brown with a golden band across the crown. The breast is a soft pink-buff; the rest of the body pale grey, with a white rear contrasting with the black tail and wing-tip. The head is rounded, with a small steel-blue bill, more like that of a goose than a duck. It is this distinctive bill that makes it easy to pick out female Wigeon amongst other surface-feeding ducks. The rest of the female's plumage is warm chestnut brown, with paler flanks.
Habitat Mudflats, estuaries, salt marshes and grassy areas near inland lakes in winter. Breeding grounds are the Arctic tundra and the sub-tundra of Scottish moors.
Nest A small depression in the ground, hidden by long grass or heather and lined with soft grass and down. Egg laying begins as

soon as the winter snows melt, which is often not until late May in the high Arctic.

Food Wigeon are grazers, feeding mainly at night on land grasses and on salt marsh and shore plants such as eel grass (*Zostera*) and duck-weed. The birds fly to and from their winter feeding grounds at dusk and dawn in tightly packed flocks, filling the air with their whistling calls.

Range The breeding range extends right across northern Europe and Asia from Iceland east to the Bering Straits.

Movements At the end of the breeding season millions of Wigeon migrate to western Europe, East Africa, north-central India and Indo-China. Most of the British winter population consists of birds from the Scandinavian breeding grounds.

RECORD OF SIGHTINGS	
Date ______	Date ______
Place ______	Place ______
Male(s) ______ Female(s) ______	Male(s) ______ Female(s) ______
Immature ______ Eclipse ______	Immature ______ Eclipse ______
Behaviour Notes	

Garganey

Anas querquedula 37–41cm **MAP 40**

Wing (M)	187–211mm	**Egg colour**	Buff
Wing (F)	182–196mm	**Clutch size**	8–9
Weight (M)	250–600g	**Incubation**	21–23 days
Weight (F)	250–550g	**Fledging**	35–40 days

Identification Garganey are about the same size as Teal, and eclipse males and females can easily be missed among a mixed flock of the two species. In summer plumage, however, the male Garganey is very distinctive, with a prominent white stripe curving over each side of the maroon-brown head to the nape. Back and breast are mottled brown, and long black and white scapulars cascade over the delicately barred pale grey flanks. The female Garganey is best identified by her distinctly striped face. Both sexes show a distinctive pale blue inner wing in flight.
Habitat Garganey breed in ponds and marshes where they are fiercely territorial. Their winter habitats are the lakes, flood rivers and deltas of Africa and southern Asia.
Nest A simple depression lined with grass and down, always located close to water.

Food Seeds, insects, larvae, crustaceans and molluscs, taken on or near the water surface as the duck swims along with neck outstretched and head partly submerged, very like the action of the Shoveler. Garganey rarely up-end.

Range Thinly distributed in western Europe (Holland, with 5000 pairs, has by far the largest population) but then more common and numerous in a broad band across eastern Europe and north-central Asia to Japan.

Movements The only Old World species to completely desert the region in winter. Garganey make journeys of thousands of miles to winter southwards from the Sahel zone in Africa, on the plains of northern India, and on the rivers and lakes of Southeast Asia.

RECORD OF SIGHTINGS	
Date ____________	Date ____________
Place ____________	Place ____________
Male(s) ______ Female(s) ______	Male(s) ______ Female(s) ______
Immature ____ Eclipse ______	Immature ____ Eclipse ______
Behaviour Notes	

Marbled Teal

Marmaronetta angustirostris 39 – 42cm **MAP 41**

Wing (M)	180 – 215mm	**Egg colour**	Yellowish
Wing (F)	174 – 206mm	**Clutch size**	7 – 14
Weight (M)	535 – 590g	**Incubation**	25 – 27 days
Weight (F)	450 – 535g	**Fledging**	?

Identification At a distance both male and female Marbled Teal appear a fairly uniform pale buff, with a darker patch around the eye. At closer quarters the plumage is seen to be boldly spotted with brown and white, but there are no strong colours or other distinctive markings. In the male a small crest at the nape makes the head appear large, and the bill too is large in both sexes. In flight, as at rest, the sexes are very similar in appearance.
Habitat The Marbled Teal is unusual in being very reluctant to commute between a safe roosting site and a good feeding ground. It requires a single habitat to provide all its needs, and is therefore restricted to shallow ponds or marsh habitats with plentiful emergent vegetation for cover and shade, and a good supply of food. Such habitats are easily converted to agricultural use, which is one probable reason for the bird's scarcity in western Europe.
Nest A shallow cup lined with grasses and down and always well hidden in dense ground vegetation close to water.
Food Uncertain. The bird feeds by dabbling at the surface and by up-ending, but authorities disagree on whether the bird is vegetarian or whether both plant and animal food is taken.

In display the male raises his crest, giving him a 'merganser-like' appearance.

Range Main stronghold in southern Europe is the Coto de Doñana in Spain, but even here numbers are dwindling, as they are in Algeria, Morocco, Tunisia and Turkey. The main breeding area is around the Caspian and Aral seas, accounting for most of the world population of between 5000 and 10,000 pairs.

Movements The species is resident in Spain, North Africa, Turkey and around the Caspian Sea, but elsewhere migrates in winter to Egypt, the Persian Gulf and Pakistan.

RECORD OF SIGHTINGS	
Date ____________	Date ____________
Place ____________	Place ____________
Male(s) ______ Female(s) ______	Male(s) ______ Female(s) ______
Immature ____ Eclipse ______	Immature ____ Eclipse ______
Behaviour Notes	

Red-crested Pochard

Netta rufina 53–57cm **MAP 42**

Wing (M)	250–273mm	**Egg colour**	Pale buff
Wing (F)	237–275mm	**Clutch size**	8–10
Weight (M)	900–1420g	**Incubation**	26–28 days
Weight (F)	830–1400g	**Fledging**	45–50 days

Identification The drake Red-crested Pochard is instantly recognizable by its bright orange-red head contrasting with the solid black of the neck, breast and underparts. The back is grey-brown, the flanks white, and the rear end black. The female lacks these bold plumage patterns and is a soft grey-brown with a darker brown cap and cream sides to the face. The male's bill is coral red; that of the female grey with a pink tip. In flight both sexes show broad white wing-bars, and these are most prominent in the black-bodied male.

Habitat The species breeds in food-rich lakes with a good surrounding growth of reeds or other vegetation, although in

Europe the birds are more adaptable than elsewhere.

Nest Made of whatever vegetation is available and lined with grass, rushes and down. The nest is always well hidden in vegetation, either on the bank or in a reed bed.

Food Mainly aquatic plants collected by diving in depths of 6 to 12 feet or by dabbling and up-ending.

Range There are scattered populations in Europe but the bird's main stronghold is around the Caspian and Aral seas and in a swathe extending eastwards across southern Siberia.

Movements The ducks leave their breeding areas to winter in the Mediterranean basin, around the Black Sea, in Iran and particularly in India, Pakistan and Bangladesh.

RECORD OF SIGHTINGS	
Date ______	Date ______
Place ______	Place ______
Male(s) ______ Female(s) ______	Male(s) ______ Female(s) ______
Immature ______ Eclipse ______	Immature ______ Eclipse ______
Behaviour Notes	

Pochard

Aythya ferina 42–49cm **MAP 43**

Wing (M)	202–223mm	**Egg colour**	Green-grey
Wing (F)	185–216mm	**Clutch size**	8–10
Weight (M)	585–1300g	**Incubation**	24–28 days
Weight (F)	467–1100g	**Fledging**	50–55 days

Identification The Pochard's closest relatives are the Canvasback and Redhead of North America, and all three are very similar in appearance. The drake Pochard has a chestnut head and neck, a black breast and rear end, and grey flanks. At a distance the head looks dark, giving a plumage pattern very like that of the Greater Scaup, but the two can be distinguished by their different head shapes. Female Pochard are mainly grey-brown, with darker brown foreparts and a pale eye-ring. Flying birds show grey wings with a paler grey wing-bar, and the species typically flies quite fast in a compact single-species flock.
Habitat Pochard breed in shallow reedy lakes and marshes across the temperate and northern zone from western Europe to eastern Siberia. They are absent from the tundra zone.

Nest A neat central cup, lined with down, in a larger structure of grasses and reeds. Built on the ground, close to water, or in dense emergent vegetation over the water.

Food The birds are mainly vegetarian, taking their food in dives to about 7 – 8 feet. They commonly feed at night and in winter spend the day sleeping on lakes and reservoirs.

Range From Iceland and Britain across to eastern Siberia. In southern Europe, scattered breeding populations occur in southern and Mediterranean Spain, Tunisia and Turkey.

Movements About one million birds winter in western Europe, the Mediterranean and Black Sea areas. The western USSR has about 380,000 and there are large winter populations in the Caspian Sea, northern India, Japan and southern China.

RECORD OF SIGHTINGS	
Date ______	Date ______
Place ______	Place ______
Male(s) ______ Female(s) ______	Male(s) ______ Female(s) ______
Immature ______ Eclipse ______	Immature ______ Eclipse ______
Behaviour Notes	

Ferruginous Duck

Aythya nyroca 38–42cm **MAP 44**

Wing (M)	180–196mm	**Egg colour**	Pale buff
Wing (F)	178–185mm	**Clutch size**	8–10
Weight (M)	440–740g	**Incubation**	25–27 days
Weight (F)	410–727g	**Fledging**	55–60 days

Identification In this species the sexes are very similar. Both have a rich dark chestnut colour over the head, neck, breast and flanks and very dark, near-black, plumage on the back. A good identification mark is the white patch of the undertail coverts. This feature is also seen in female Tufted Duck, especially in autumn, but the Ferruginous Duck's high peaked crown is quite unlike the rounded crown of the Tufted so confusion should be avoided. At close quarters the male Ferruginous Duck is distinguished from the female by his pale eye and dark neck-ring.

Habitat Ferruginous Duck breed only on shallow fresh waters with abundant aquatic plant growth and dense emergent vegetation such as reeds and willows. Outside the breeding season both saline habitats and more open habitats are used.

Nest A thick platform, hidden among emergent or floating vegetation, built from whatever material is available.
Food Mainly seeds, leaves and plant stems. About half the food is taken by diving, the rest by dabbling.
Range The bird's main stronghold lies between, and north of, the Black and Caspian seas. Also south and east of the Aral Sea. It breeds in east Europe but is rare and scattered farther west. Small and dwindling populations exist in France and Spain, but the species is no longer seen regularly in Italy, Greece, Morocco or Algeria.
Movements Most birds winter in the south of the Black Sea-Caspian Sea area, or in Turkey, Italy and parts of North Africa. More easterly populations migrate to northern India.

RECORD OF SIGHTINGS	
Date ____	Date ____
Place ____	Place ____
Male(s) ____ Female(s) ____	Male(s) ____ Female(s) ____
Immature ____ Eclipse ____	Immature ____ Eclipse ____
Behaviour Notes	

Tufted Duck

Aythya fuligula 40–47cm **MAP 45**

Wing (M)	194–215mm	**Egg colour**	Green-grey
Wing (F)	185–205mm	**Clutch size**	8–11
Weight (M)	475–1028g	**Incubation**	23–28 days
Weight (F)	335–995g	**Fledging**	45–50 days

Identification The male Tufted Duck is a neat, attractive little bird with head, breast and back a glossy black and the head washed with purple. Flanks and undersides are pure white. The bill is silver-grey with a black tip, the eye is orange-yellow, and the back of the head is adorned with a small drooping crest. Most other black and white species have angular heads: the Tufted is distinguished by its delicately rounded head. The female is chocolate-brown with paler flanks barred with buff. In flight both sexes show a prominent white wing-bar against the otherwise dark plumage.

Habitat Medium-depth freshwater lakes, flooded gravel pits and reservoirs. The bird's dramatic expansion across north and west

Europe in the last 100 years is largely due to its liking for the lowland reservoirs that have been built.

Nest A shallow cup of dry grass, reeds and leaves, often on an island or on a large grass tussock in marshland. Usually well concealed, but occasionally in the open if the duck is nesting in the middle of a gull or tern colony.

Food Molluscs, insects, crustaceans and some seeds, taken mainly by diving but also by dabbling and up-ending.

Range Iceland, British Isles, patchily across Northwest Europe, then right across Eurasia to Kamchatka and Japan.

Movements Rafts of up to 2000 Tufteds bobbing on the choppy waves of reservoirs in winter are an increasingly common sight in Europe. Elsewhere the birds winter in East Africa, the Caspian Sea, northern India, southern China and Japan.

RECORD OF SIGHTINGS	
Date ________________	Date ________________
Place ________________	Place ________________
Male(s) ______ Female(s) ______	Male(s) ______ Female(s) ______
Immature ____ Eclipse ______	Immature ____ Eclipse ______
Behaviour Notes	

Smew

Mergus albellus 38–44cm **MAP 46**

Wing (M)	188–208mm	**Egg colour**	Creamy buff
Wing (F)	171–189mm	**Clutch size**	7–9
Weight (M)	510–935g	**Incubation**	26–28 days
Weight (F)	500–680g	**Fledging**	?

Identification The male Smew is a brilliant white bird with bold black lines over the back, a black mask, and a large white erectile crest running from the forehead over the crown. Its colouring is quite unique, and but for its characteristic duck shape it might be mistaken for a small gull. The female is dark grey above and slightly paler on the flanks and breast. The cheeks are white, the crown a deep rust colour. Young birds of both sexes look very like females, and all are referred to collectively as 'redheads'.
Habitat Smew breed on small ponds and lakes throughout the northern forest zone south of the tundra, and winter on ice-free lakes and reservoirs and coastal bays and estuaries.
Nest Usually a tree-hole (often that of a Black Woodpecker) though Smew will also use nest boxes erected for Goldeneye.

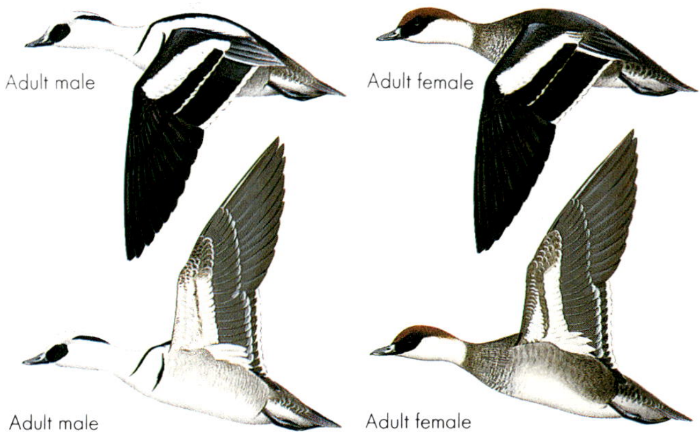

Food Mainly fish, often caught by diving among the ice of a part-frozen lake or reservoir. The winter diet includes carp, eels, young salmon and minnows. In spring and summer, insects and larvae (notably caddisfly larvae) are important foods.
Range Smew breed from northern Scandinavia east across the boreal zone to the Sea of Okhotsk, and in Kamchatka.
Movements These far northern birds are seen in temperate regions only as winter visitors. Their short take-off abilities enable them to use small, iced-over ponds and backwaters shunned by other species. Wintering grounds are scattered across Europe, around the Caspian Sea, and in China and Japan.

RECORD OF SIGHTINGS	
Date ______	Date ______
Place ______	Place ______
Male(s) ______ Female(s) ______	Male(s) ______ Female(s) ______
Immature ______ Eclipse ______	Immature ______ Eclipse ______
Behaviour Notes	

White-headed Duck

Oxyura leucocephala 43–48cm **MAP 47**

Wing (M)	157–172mm	**Egg colour**	White
Wing (F)	148–167mm	**Clutch size**	5–10
Weight (M)	720–800g	**Incubation**	25–26 days
Weight (F)	510–900g	**Fledging**	?

Identification The drake is buff-brown, heavily barred on the flanks and back, and has a white face and head with a dark centre to the crown. The bill is large, bulbous, and blue in colour. Females are duller overall, with more pronounced barring, and have a distinctive light band across the otherwise dark grey face. The bill too is dark grey. The face pattern is similar to that of the female Ruddy Duck but is much more pronounced. In flight the species is identified by the completely uniform wing colour and long pointed tail.

Habitat Like most of the stiff-tailed ducks, the White-head prefers shallow waters with abundant floating and emergent vegetation. The species' current scarcity is probably partly due to the suitability of such habitats for 'reclamation'.

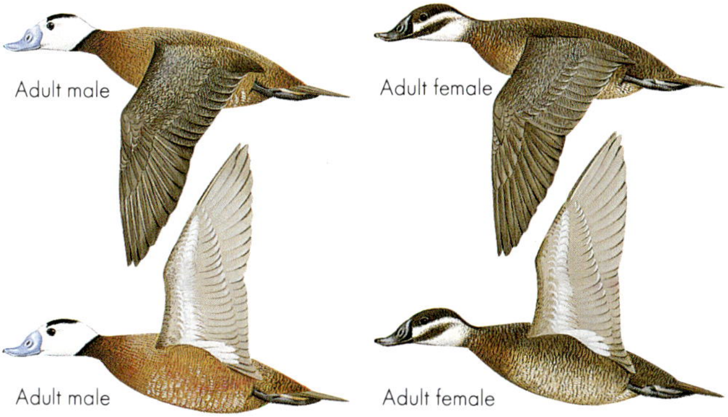

Nest A platform built of aquatic vegetation, often using the remains of an old nest as a base.
Food White-heads are omnivores, feeding on seeds and leaves for much of the year but also taking insects when plentiful, and snails, worms and crustaceans in winter. Even in shallow water the birds typically make prolonged dives.
Range Current breeding range is reduced to scattered sites in Spain, North Africa and Turkey, and the steppe region of the southern USSR, notably in Kazakhstan.
Movements Despite not being strong fliers, White-heads make quite long journeys. Over 1000 winter in Pakistan, 800 on the Caspian Sea and 1000 in Tunisia, but the main concentration is the 6000 – 9000 winter population of Burdur Gölü in Turkey.

RECORD OF SIGHTINGS	
Date ______	Date ______
Place ______	Place ______
Male(s) ____ Female(s) ____	Male(s) ____ Female(s) ____
Immature ____ Eclipse ____	Immature ____ Eclipse ____
Behaviour Notes	

Ducks of North America and Asia

Fulvous Whistling Duck

Drendrocygna bicolor 51 – 53cm **MAP 34**

Wing (M)	209 – 220mm	**Egg colour**	White
Wing (F)	212 – 220mm	**Clutch size**	6 – 16
Weight (M)	*c* 747g	**Incubation**	24 – 26 days
Weight (F)	590 – 770g	**Fledging**	63 days

Identification As its name implies, the Fulvous Whistling Duck is a rich orange-brown on the head, breast and underparts. There is a distinctive pale goose-like flash on the throat, and the upperparts are dark brown with bold tawny barring. Like other whistling ducks the Fulvous has long strong legs, which in this species are blue-grey in colour. A useful identification clue to the whistling ducks is that the legs extend well beyond the tail in flight, giving the birds a characteristically long-tailed appearance. Male and female can usually be separated only by their calls. The birds are gregarious in habit and typically stand very upright in tightly packed groups.

Habitat The species is essentially a marshland bird and has adapted well to rice-fields, especially in the US. The alternative name Tree Duck is widely used in many parts of the bird's range.

Adult male and female are virtually identical in flight and on the ground.

Nest A simple cup placed among emergent marsh vegetation, usually over water. In some areas the birds nest in tree-holes, on the ground, or in disused nests of other species.
Food Seeds of water plants, grain, and aquatic insects (particularly beetles) taken while diving.
Range One of the most extraordinary distributions of any bird. The species occurs in the southern US and Mexico, South America, sub-Saharan Africa, Madagascar, India, Sri Lanka and Burma – with no distinguishable variation.
Movements Like most tropical species the Fulvous Whistling Duck is a year-round resident.

RECORD OF SIGHTINGS	
Date ____________	Date ____________
Place ____________	Place ____________
Male(s) ______ Female(s) ______	Male(s) ______ Female(s) ______
Immature ____ Eclipse ______	Immature ____ Eclipse ______
Behaviour Notes	

Black-bellied Whistling Duck

Dendrocygna autumnalis 51–56cm **MAP 1**

Wing (M)	231–251mm	**Egg colour**	Buff-white
Wing (F)	223–249mm	**Clutch size**	12–16
Weight (M)	728–951g	**Incubation**	25–31 days
Weight (F)	831–978g	**Fledging**	56 days

Identification As with most whistling ducks, the sexes are virtually identical both on the ground and in flight. The crown, nape, lower neck, breast and back are all uniformly brown. The underparts are black, and are separated from the upperparts by a broad slash of white formed by the white plumage of the folded forewing. The sides of the face and the throat are grey-buff, and the bill is bright red, hence the species' alternative name of Red-billed Whistling Duck. The legs are long, and bright pink, and the stance is typically upright with the neck stretched upwards. In the air both sexes display a white forewing with contrasting black trailing edge, and uniformly dark belly and underwing.

Habitat Mainly shallow marshes, where the bird spends much of its time wading, usually in the company of others. Where trees and bushes are available nearby, the birds regularly perch among the branches.

Nest The birds lay their eggs in unlined tree-holes, close to water. Holes in ebony and hackberry are favoured, but nest-boxes are also used, and birds will occasionally nest on the ground among thick vegetation.

Adult male and female are virtually identical in flight and on the ground.

Like other whistling ducks the Black-bellied often stands upright, especially when curious or alarmed.

Food Seeds, roots and tubers of aquatic plants, gathered by diving and by up-ending. Also insects and molluscs.
Range The northern subspecies, reviewed here, is found from the Canal Zone north to Mexico and southwestern Texas, though records from Arizona and New Mexico suggest an expanding range. The southern subspecies ranges south to Argentina.
Movements Though basically resident, some birds do draw back from the limits of their range in winter.

RECORD OF SIGHTINGS	
Date ______	Date ______
Place ______	Place ______
Male(s) ______ Female(s) ______	Male(s) ______ Female(s) ______
Immature ______ Eclipse ______	Immature ______ Eclipse ______
Behaviour Notes	

Wood Duck

Aix sponsa 43–51cm **MAP 2**

Wing (M)	218–240mm	**Egg colour**	Whitish
Wing (F)	211–231mm	**Clutch size**	9–14
Weight (M)	*c* 681g	**Incubation**	31–35 days
Weight (F)	*c* 635g	**Fledging**	56–63 days

Identification The drake Wood Duck rivals even his close relative the Mandarin for spectacular colours and patterns. A bright orange-red bill and eye are set in a near-black head marked with bold stripes of white and topped by a large curving crest of iridescent green. The breast is chestnut spotted with white, the flanks are a buff yellow and the back bottle green. In flight the dark upper wing shows a deep blue speculum. The female is less gaudy but also attractive with soft brown underparts spotted with buff, a white eye-ring, and grey-green upperparts marked by a blue speculum like that of the male.

Habitat Wood Duck inhabit small ponds and rivers in thickly wooded country and are rarely seen on large stretches of open

water. They are true woodland birds, never far from the trees that provide their roosting and nesting sites.

Nest A tree-hole, often that of a Pileated Woodpecker, with a lining of down that accumulates from the duck's preening and not from deliberate plucking. The hole entrance must be about 4.5in across and the cavity at least two feet deep.

Food Mainly plant food obtained by dabbling and also by up-ending. Also grazes on waterside vegetation.

Range Wood Duck breed on both sides of the Rockies and over much of the eastern half of North America but are absent from the largely treeless plains and the arid southwest.

Movements Birds in the extreme north of the range migrate south in winter, though some do winter as far north as New York State.

RECORD OF SIGHTINGS	
Date ______	Date ______
Place ______	Place ______
Male(s) ______ Female(s) ______	Male(s) ______ Female(s) ______
Immature ______ Eclipse ______	Immature ______ Eclipse ______
Behaviour Notes	

American Wigeon

Anas americana 45–56cm **MAP 3**

Wing (M)	256–275mm	**Egg colour**	Cream
Wing (F)	236–256mm	**Clutch size**	8–10
Weight (M)	650–1135g	**Incubation**	*c* 23 days
Weight (F)	510–825g	**Fledging**	45–63 days

Identification The overall plumage pattern of this American species is very like that of its close European relative, but instead of a bold golden stripe over the top of the head the American drake has a yellow-white crown. The rest of the head plumage is mottled grey-brown, with a bold slash of bottle green running from the eye to the nape. Breast and back are buff-pink, the belly white and the rear end black. The female is even more similar to the European species, with warm brown colouring, a slightly greyer head, but the same neat rounded crown and small upturned bill. In flight too both sexes are very like the European Wigeon: the male with a white forewing and contrasting dark speculum, the female with brown upper wing and dark speculum.

Habitat Breeds on small lakes and marshes in open and lightly wooded country. Winters in freshwater marshlands.
Nest A hollow on the ground at the edge of a lake or on an island, usually well hidden in reeds and lined with down.
Food Mainly plant food obtained by dabbling or by grazing on lakeside grassland, often in large tightly-packed flocks.
Range The bird breeds in a broad zone from central Alaska eastwards to Maine and southwards through the Rockies and prairies to northeastern California and northern New Mexico.
Movements At the end of the breeding season the entire population flies south to winter along the mild southern shores of the US or in Central America and the West Indies.

RECORD OF SIGHTINGS	
Date ______	Date ______
Place ______	Place ______
Male(s) ______ Female(s) ______	Male(s) ______ Female(s) ______
Immature ____ Eclipse ______	Immature ____ Eclipse ______
Behaviour Notes	

Black Duck

Anas rubripes 56 – 66cm **MAP 4**

Wing (M)	265 – 301mm	**Egg colour**	Grey-green
Wing (F)	245 – 275mm	**Clutch size**	7 – 11
Weight (M)	905 – 1730g	**Incubation**	27 – 33 days
Weight (F)	850 – 1330g	**Fledging**	50 – 56 days

Identification Black Duck are unusual among the surface-feeding species in that male and female birds are almost identical. Sexual dimorphism is limited to different bill-colours – yellow in the male, olive-grey in the female. Both male and female Black Duck closely resemble female Mallard. The body plumage consists of dark brown feathers edged with buff, the crown is dark, and there is a dark stripe running through the eye, contrasting with the paler feathers covering the sides of the face and the neck. The upper wing is dark with a deep purple speculum; the underwing white in marked contrast to the dark body. Legs are orange-red.
Habitat Breeds on freshwater and saltwater marshes, often in wooded country. Also on small offshore islands. Winters on estuaries, and in coastal marshlands and sheltered bays.

Nest A simple hollow lined with grass, twigs and down. The nest may be on the ground among dense tussocks, under a bush, beneath a rotten stump or pile of brushwood, or in a tree-hole or the abandoned nest of another bird.
Food Plant food gathered by dabbling and up-ending, by wading in shallow water, and by grazing on land.
Range Totally North American. The bird breeds in eastern Canada from Hudson Bay across to Newfoundland and then south to the Great Lakes and down the coast to North Carolina.
Movements In winter most birds move to the southeastern states, Florida and the Gulf Coast, but summer and winter ranges overlap considerably, and Black Duck are the dominant winter duck from New England north to Newfoundland.

RECORD OF SIGHTINGS	
Date ______	Date ______
Place ______	Place ______
Male(s) ____ Female(s) ____	Male(s) ____ Female(s) ____
Immature ____ Eclipse ____	Immature ____ Eclipse ____
Behaviour Notes	

Blue-winged Teal

Anas discors 37 – 41cm **MAP 5**

Wing (M)	186 – 195mm	**Egg colour**	Buff
Wing (F)	176 – 188mm	**Clutch size**	9 – 13
Weight (M)	290 – 499g	**Incubation**	23 – 24 days
Weight (F)	280 – 492g	**Fledging**	*c* 42 days

Identification The Blue-winged Teal is the North American equivalent of the Old World Garganey, and like that species the drake has an immediately diagnostic face pattern. The head is slate-blue marked by a bold white crescent curving in front of the eye. The body plumage is warm buff heavily spotted with dark brown, the flanks are white and the rear end black. The female is very like the Green-winged Teal but slightly darker with a more pronounced stripe through the eye and a pale spot at the base of the bill. In flight both sexes show a pale blue inner forewing.

Habitat Marshes and shallow freshwater lakes with abundant emergent plant growth, in open country and on the coast. Winters on lakes and coastal lagoons and in mangrove swamps.

Nest A bare hollow on the ground. No down is added until several eggs have been laid.
Food Mainly grass seeds and waterweed leaves, gathered by dabbling and only rarely by up-ending. Molluscs, insects and crustaceans are also eaten. The birds are shy, often feeding in small groups, close inshore under cover of vegetation.
Range Blue-winged Teal breed in a broad zone across boreal and temperate North America from southern Alaska and the St Lawrence river south to Nevada, Texas and North Carolina.
Movements Summer and winter ranges have little overlap. In winter the birds migrate to Baja California, the Gulf Coast, Mexico, the West Indies and south to Colombia and Venezuela.

RECORD OF SIGHTINGS	
Date ______	Date ______
Place ______	Place ______
Male(s) ______ Female(s) ______	Male(s) ______ Female(s) ______
Immature ______ Eclipse ______	Immature ______ Eclipse ______
Behaviour Notes	

Cinnamon Teal

Anas cyanoptera 38–43cm **MAP 6**

Wing (M)	184–197mm	**Egg colour**	Pale buff
Wing (F)	170–187mm	**Clutch size**	*c* 9
Weight (M)	?	**Incubation**	?
Weight (F)	?	**Fledging**	?

Identification The male Cinnamon Teal is a rich deep chestnut colour on head, neck, breast and underparts, and brown patterned with buff on the upperparts. The female is very similar to the female Blue-winged Teal even at fairly close range, having the same buff plumage heavily spotted with brown though with a less pronounced pale patch at the base of the bill. Male and female also have a pale blue inner forewing like that of the Blue-winged Teal.
Habitat Shallow marshes and the margins of pools in open country and mountain areas. A single subspecies inhabits the western USA;

Adult male

Adult male

four more subspecies are found in South America, ranging from the lowlands to the high Andean plateau lakes.

Nest Hidden among ground cover, usually close to water.

Food Mainly seeds and plant stems, but the diet includes small molluscs and insects. Food is taken at the water surface by dabbling. As in the Shoveler, small food items are collected by straining the water through the well-developed lamellae along the bill margins.

Range Cinnamon Teal breed in western North America from southern British Columbia through Washington and Montana south to California and throughout Mexico.

Movements Southern breeding birds are mainly resident; those breeding farther north migrate in early autumn to wintering grounds in California and Mexico.

RECORD OF SIGHTINGS	
Date ______	Date ______
Place ______	Place ______
Male(s) ____ Female(s) ____	Male(s) ____ Female(s) ____
Immature ____ Eclipse ____	Immature ____ Eclipse ____
Behaviour Notes	

Canvasback

Aythya valisineria 50 – 58cm **MAP 7**

Wing (M)	229 – 248mm	**Egg colour**	Olive-grey
Wing (F)	221 – 234mm	**Clutch size**	*c* 10
Weight (M)	850 – 1600	**Incubation**	23 – 29 days
Weight (F)	950 – 1390g	**Fledging**	60 – 70 days

Identification The Canvasback is the largest member of the 'Pochard' group. The drake is a large bird with rust-red head, black breast and rear end, and a grey-white back. The neck is long and the bill substantial, which helps to distinguish the species from the similarly patterned Redhead, Pochard and Greater and Lesser Scaup. The forehead slopes into the bill giving a wedge-shaped profile to the head which is one of the best identifying features. The female is very similar to the female Redhead, though the head shape is distinctive.
Habitat Breeds on prairie marshes and shallow lakes with abundant marginal vegetation. Winters on open lakes, and on coastal lagoons, estuaries and bays.

Nest A platform of aquatic vegetation built among waterside plants, often over shallow water. If the nest floods, the female adds more plant material to raise the level of the cup.
Food Mainly seeds, leaves and tubers of aquatic plants, but some animal food is also taken. The birds feed morning and evening, diving and dabbling in small flocks and spending much of the day resting and sleeping well out on open water.
Range The species breeds over much of northwestern North America, from Alaska south through northwestern Canada, the eastern Rockies and prairies to Iowa.
Movements After breeding, the whole population moves south to winter along the coast from British Columbia to Baja California and from Mexico round the east coast to Cape Cod.

RECORD OF SIGHTINGS	
Date ______	Date ______
Place ______	Place ______
Male(s) ______ Female(s) ______	Male(s) ______ Female(s) ______
Immature ______ Eclipse ______	Immature ______ Eclipse ______
Behaviour Notes	

Redhead

Aythya americana 50–52cm **MAP 8**

Wing (M)	231–240mm	**Egg colour**	Creamy white
Wing (F)	210–230mm	**Clutch size**	*c* 9
Weight (M)	900–1400g	**Incubation**	23–29 days
Weight (F)	900–990g	**Fledging**	60–65 days

Identification The drake Redhead is a distinctive bird with a chestnut head and neck, glossy black breast, and grey back and flanks. Only two other North American diving ducks have chestnut heads – the Canvasback, whose range widely overlaps that of the Redhead, and the rare Pochard, which is known only from a handful of sightings in the Aleutian Islands. The Redhead is best distinguished by its rounded head and steep forehead – a profile quite unlike the sloping outline of the Pochard or the wedge-like shape of the Canvasback's head and bill. Female Redheads are brownish-grey with paler throat and neck, and both sexes have silver-grey or blue-grey bills tipped with black.

Habitat Breeds on shallow freshwater lakes and marshes in open country. Winters mainly in coastal waters, on brackish lagoons, sheltered bays and tidal marshes.

Nest Some females build a nest in waterside vegetation, some lay eggs in other ducks' nests and then lay again in nests of their own, while some are entirely parasitic.
Food Plant and animal food collected mainly by diving but also by dabbling. The birds feed actively in the morning and evening, resting by day on open waters on lakes or at sea.
Range Redheads breed over a huge area of middle and western North America from California north to the Great Slave Lake and eastwards to Minnesota. Since the 1950s a breeding population has also become established in central Alaska.
Movements In winter the birds migrate south and east to winter on salt lakes, saline marshes and sea coasts from California around the Gulf Coast and north to Cape Cod.

RECORD OF SIGHTINGS	
Date ______	Date ______
Place ______	Place ______
Male(s) ______ Female(s) ______	Male(s) ______ Female(s) ______
Immature ____ Eclipse ______	Immature ____ Eclipse ______
Behaviour Notes	

Ring-necked Duck

Aythya collaris 37 – 46cm **MAP 9**

Wing (M)	194 – 206mm	**Egg colour**	Olive
Wing (F)	185 – 201mm	**Clutch size**	6 – 14
Weight (M)	681 – 937g	**Incubation**	25 – 29 days
Weight (F)	511 – 879g	**Fledging**	49 – 55 days

Identification The drake Ring-neck is a predominantly black and white bird though at close quarters the head and neck are seen to be washed with purple and the breast with green. Upperparts and rear are black, and the pale grey flanks are separated from the dark breast by a bold crescent of white. The bird is distinguished from the otherwise similar Tufted Duck by the characteristic high crown, by the banding on the steel-grey bill, and by a white wedge below the bend of the wing. The female is identified by the same angular head shape and by the pale eye-ring and stripe. In flight both sexes show grey wing-bars.

Habitat Breeds on marshes and on very shallow lakes and ponds in open lowland country. Winters mainly on freshwater lakes but also locally on brackish coastal lagoons and bays.

Nest The first eggs are laid in a bare scrape, after which some grass and a lining of down are added.
Food Mainly seeds, pondweeds and tubers of aquatic plants taken by dabbling and occasional up-ending. Insect larvae, molluscs, worms and crustaceans may account for up to one-fifth of the total food intake.
Range Ring-necked Duck breed across the northern and temperate zone of Canada but are absent from the prairies. In the US the range includes Dakota, Minnesota, Wisconsin and Maine. Since 1960 the species has also bred in Alaska.
Movements The birds winter all round the US coastline but for the extreme northeast, and in Mexico and the West Indies. Vagrants have been recorded in Britain and several other European countries, and in Hawaii and Venezuela.

RECORD OF SIGHTINGS	
Date ______	Date ______
Place ______	Place ______
Male(s) ______ Female(s) ______	Male(s) ______ Female(s) ______
Immature ____ Eclipse ______	Immature ____ Eclipse ______
Behaviour Notes	

Lesser Scaup

Aythya affinis 42–47cm **MAP 10**

Wing (M)	194–208mm	**Egg colour**	Olive-buff
Wing (F)	191–202mm	**Clutch size**	9–11
Weight (M)	620–1050g	**Incubation**	21–22 days
Weight (F)	540–960g	**Fledging**	47–54 days

Identification Though slightly smaller than its close relative the Greater Scaup, the Lesser is almost identical and must be distinguished carefully on details. The drake has a black head, neck and breast with a purple sheen. The rear end is black and the flanks and back grey. The female, like the female Greater, is brown with barred flanks and a white face. The birds are best distinguished at close range by the slight crest that creates a peak towards the rear of the crown. The high point on the head of the Greater Scaup is well forward. In flight the Lesser's white wing-bar fades to grey on the outer wing, giving the impression of a white speculum, while that of the Greater is white to the wing-tip.
Habitat Marshes, freshwater pools and lakes in the tundra zone

and the northern prairies. Winters on lowland lakes and in coastal lagoons, bays and estuaries.

Nest A simple hollow among vegetation, usually close to water. The eggs are laid on a bed of grass, and down is added later as the clutch increases in size.

Food The diet consists largely of small crustaceans caught by diving. Lesser Scaup show a strong preference for freshwater habitats and shallow water depths.

Range From central Alaska across northern Canada to Hudson Bay, and south to Michigan, the Dakotas and Montana.

Movements The birds desert their summer range to winter in a broad sweep across the southern US and south through Mexico, Central America, the West Indies and Venezuela.

RECORD OF SIGHTINGS	
Date ______	Date ______
Place ______	Place ______
Male(s) ______ Female(s) ______	Male(s) ______ Female(s) ______
Immature ____ Eclipse ______	Immature ____ Eclipse ______
Behaviour Notes	

Spectacled Eider

Somateria fischeri 52 – 57cm **MAP 24**

Wing (M)	225 – 280mm	**Egg colour**	Olive-grey
Wing (F)	233 – 280mm	**Clutch size**	5 – 6
Weight (M)	1500 – 1850g	**Incubation**	?
Weight (F)	1400 – 1850g	**Fledging**	?

Identification The drake Spectacled Eider is every bit as distinctive as its three close relatives. Identifying it is not a problem: seeing one might be, as this is one of the most geographically restricted of all ducks. The male is slate-black below and white above, and the head pattern is dominated by huge white eye-patches bordered with black, and by a cloak of long green feathers covering the crown and nape. The orange bill is partly covered by a second cloak of pale green feathers, bordered with white. Females and juvenile males are reddish-brown with prominent dark barring, and both have dark blue-grey bills.

Habitat Spectacled Eider breed on coastal tundra and on pools and streams up to 75 miles inland. They are thought to winter at sea along the edge of the pack-ice zone.
Nest A substantial pile of grassy stems, usually placed on a tussock or ridge not far from open water. Initially quite open but later screened as surrounding vegetation grows up.
Food In summer the birds feed extensively on insects and their larvae; in winter they dive for marine molluscs.
Range Breeding range is the coastal strip at either side of the Yukon delta in Alaska, and the Siberian coast between, and including, the estuaries of the Kolyma and Indigirka.
Movements The birds are thought to winter in the shallower waters of the Bering Sea, probably to the north of Kamchatka.

RECORD OF SIGHTINGS	
Date ________	Date ________
Place ________	Place ________
Male(s) ______ Female(s) ______	Male(s) ______ Female(s) ______
Immature ____ Eclipse ______	Immature ____ Eclipse ______
Behaviour Notes	

Surf Scoter

Melanitta perspicillata 45 – 56cm **MAP 11**

Wing (M)	238 – 256mm	**Egg colour**	Cream
Wing (F)	223 – 235mm	**Clutch size**	5 – 7
Weight (M)	652 – 1134g	**Incubation**	?
Weight (F)	680 – 992g	**Fledging**	?

Identification The male Surf Scoter is completely black but for the bold white markings on the front of the head and on the nape. The bill is a mosaic of white, red, yellow and black and this feature, plus the unique head pattern, makes the bird quite unmistakable at close quarters. Unlike the Velvet Scoter there is no white in the wing. In flight the bird is very like the Common Scoter but the wing-beats are rather slower. The female of the species is dark brown with pale markings on the face. She may thus be confused with the female Velvet Scoter or the female Harlequin, but can be distinguished from these birds by the long straight eider-like profile of the head and bill.

Habitat In summer the birds live by lakes, pools and river-banks in thinly wooded country. Winter is spent in coastal waters, especially in shallow bays and estuaries.
Nest A bed of grass and down, well hidden among long grass or under a low bush, and often some distance from water.
Food In summer insects and plant food are important parts of the diet. In winter the birds feed at sea on molluscs, crustaceans and fish eggs when these are abundant.
Range The birds breed in a broad sweep across the northern zone from western and northern Alaska to Hudson Bay, and in a separate area in central Labrador.
Movements Most Surf Scoter move from the interior to the coast in winter, and are found from the Aleutians to Baja California on the west coast and from Nova Scotia to South Carolina in the east.

RECORD OF SIGHTINGS	
Date ______	Date ______
Place ______	Place ______
Male(s) ______ Female(s) ______	Male(s) ______ Female(s) ______
Immature ____ Eclipse ______	Immature ____ Eclipse ______
Behaviour Notes	

Bufflehead

Bucephala albeola 32–39cm **MAP 12**

Wing (M)	169–179mm	**Egg colour**	Creamy buff
Wing (F)	151–161mm	**Clutch size**	6–11
Weight (M)	270–600g	**Incubation**	29–31 days
Weight (F)	230–470g	**Fledging**	50–55 days

Identification The Bufflehead is a small version of the Goldeneye which dives well, swims high in the water and flies on fast-beating wings. The drake is black above and white below, with a broad white band running around the back of the head to end at the eye at either side. The head often shows a purple or bronze sheen. The female is dark brown above and barred buff below, with a bold comma-shaped patch of white on the cheek. In flight, the female's white speculum and the white inner wings of the male are particularly prominent.

Habitat Small pools, lakes and slow-running streams in the mixed forest zone south of the tundra. The birds winter on large inland freshwater lakes, coastal bays and estuaries.

Nest A tree-hole, always close to water and often used for several consecutive years. Holes of Yellow-shafted Flickers are commonly used, and a sparse lining of down is added after the first eggs have been laid.
Food Insects and larvae in summer, with some seeds and plant stems. Mainly molluscs and crustaceans in winter.
Range From Alaska eastwards across Canada to north-central Quebec and south to the US border. Farther south Bufflehead breed only locally in a few parts of the western US.
Movements Bufflehead winter on the coast in the west from the Aleutians to Baja California, through Mexico and the Gulf Coast, and down the east coast from Nova Scotia to Florida. Wintering birds are also found inland, in a band stretching from the Great Lakes south to Louisiana.

RECORD OF SIGHTINGS	
Date ______	Date ______
Place ______	Place ______
Male(s) ____ Female(s) ____	Male(s) ____ Female(s) ____
Immature ____ Eclipse ____	Immature ____ Eclipse ____
Behaviour Notes	

Barrow's Goldeneye

Bucephala islandica 42–53cm **MAP 13**

Wing (M)	229–248mm	**Egg colour**	Blue-green
Wing (F)	211–221mm	**Clutch size**	8–11
Weight (M)	1191–1304g	**Incubation**	28–30 days
Weight (F)	737–907g	**Fledging**	?

Identification At first glance the male Barrow's Goldeneye is very like the closely related Common Goldeneye but there are three key differences. In Barrow's the head has a purple sheen rather than green, the white patch on the face is crescent-shaped rather than round, and the pattern on the back is more dominantly black than in the Common Goldeneye. Even in flight, Barrow's is, overall, a much darker bird. The female is even more difficult to identify. The forehead is almost vertical and the head rounded, but otherwise the duck is identical to the female Common Goldeneye.
Habitat Clear still lakes, fast streams and torrents in summer. Winter is spent along ice-free rivers and lakes and in coastal waters and estuaries.

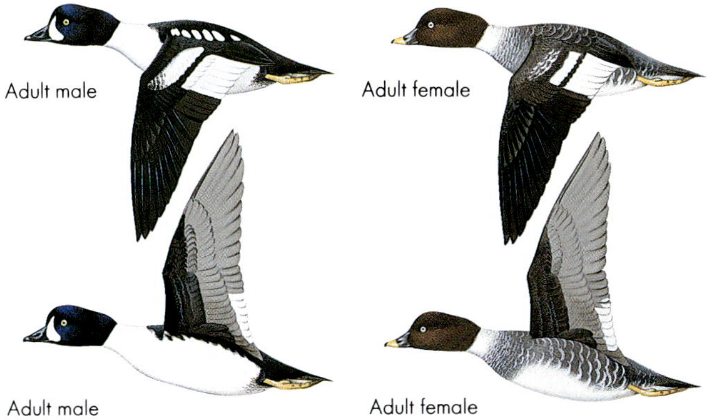

Nest Tree-holes, usually those abandoned by Pileated Woodpeckers or Yellow-shafted Flickers, nearly always close to water. In Iceland and other largely treeless areas the birds nest among ground vegetation or in rock crevices.
Food In summer the main foods are insects and larvae, especially caddisfly larvae and dragonfly nymphs, plus molluscs, and the seeds and leaves of pondweeds. The winter diet consists mainly of molluscs and crustaceans.
Range Southern Alaska to Washington State and scattered locations farther south, then a huge gap to Labrador and outposts in southwestern Greenland and in Iceland.
Movements Barrow's Goldeneye travel no farther than the nearest ice-free coast and are therefore rarely seen as vagrants.

RECORD OF SIGHTINGS	
Date ______	Date ______
Place ______	Place ______
Male(s) ____ Female(s) ____	Male(s) ____ Female(s) ____
Immature ____ Eclipse ____	Immature ____ Eclipse ____
Behaviour Notes	

Hooded Merganser

Mergus cucullatus 42–50cm **MAP 14**

Wing (M)	193–202mm	**Egg colour**	White
Wing (F)	184–198mm	**Clutch size**	8–12
Weight (M)	595–879g	**Incubation**	29–37 days
Weight (F)	453–652g	**Fledging**	*c* 71 days

Identification Much the smallest of the American sawbilled ducks, the Hooded Merganser takes its name from the male's large black and white fan-shaped crest. The drake is black above and cinnamon below, with a white breast, bright yellow eye and a thin black bill. With the crest lowered the head appears rectangular and black with a white slash along the side. With the crest raised the head appears huge, and the whole side of the head is white, tipped with black. The female is grey-brown below and grey above, with a less conspicuous orange-buff crest. In flight both sexes show only a narrow white bar on the inner wing, so a dark-winged sawbill is most likely to be this species.

Habitat Hooded Mergansers breed on small ponds, marshes and backwaters surrounded by forest. Winter is spent in similar habitats and on quiet estuaries, lagoons and mangroves.
Nest A down-lined hole in a tree, usually in or close to water; often an old woodpecker hole enlarged by decay. Where nest-sites are scarce, a single hole may be used by more than one duck.
Food Up to 60 percent crayfish and aquatic insects; the balance made up of small fish, all taken by diving.
Range British Columbia to Washington in the west, and from Manitoba and Nova Scotia south to Louisiana in the east. Always in wooded country; absent from the prairie lands.
Movements While the western population winters mainly on the local coastline, eastern birds migrate south to the Gulf Coast, Florida and Louisiana.

RECORD OF SIGHTINGS	
Date ______	Date ______
Place ______	Place ______
Male(s) ______ Female(s) ______	Male(s) ______ Female(s) ______
Immature ____ Eclipse ______	Immature ____ Eclipse ______
Behaviour Notes	

Masked Duck

Oxyura dominica 33–39cm **MAP 15**

Wing (M)	142–148mm	**Egg colour**	Buff
Wing (F)	136–148mm	**Clutch size**	4–8
Weight (M)	323–395g	**Incubation**	?
Weight (F)	345–391g	**Fledging**	?

Identification This species, also called the White-winged Lake Duck, is a tropical American member of the stifftail tribe which has spread into North America in the last 100 years. The drake has a distinctive black mask covering the entire face and crown. The neck and body are rich chestnut and the back and flanks are boldly spotted with black. The bill is large and bright blue with a broad black tip and a pronounced nail. The female is dark brown above with buff markings, pale buff below with dark brown mottling. The crown is dark brown and the pale face is crossed by two dark bands, one through the eye, the other crossing the cheek.

Habitat Swamps and marshes with extensive stands of dense emergent vegetation broken by stretches of open water. The bird is shy and skulking, and therefore difficult to see.
Nest A neat cup of grasses, often sited amongst reeds but also often in rice fields.
Food Feeds on water plants, mainly by diving.
Range Tropical northern South America from Argentina north to Central America, the West Indies, Mexico and, since 1870, the southwestern corner of Texas.
Movements Like most tropical species the Masked Duck is not strongly migratory but the species does disperse at times and vagrants have been recorded as far north as Wisconsin, Massachusetts and Vermont and east to North Carolina.

RECORD OF SIGHTINGS	
Date ______	Date ______
Place ______	Place ______
Male(s) ______ Female(s) ______	Male(s) ______ Female(s) ______
Immature ______ Eclipse ______	Immature ______ Eclipse ______
Behaviour Notes	

Falcated Teal

Anas falcata 48–54cm **MAP 48**

Wing (M)	253–264mm	**Egg colour**	Yellowish
Wing (F)	237–249mm	**Clutch size**	*c* 8
Weight (M)	590–770g	**Incubation**	*c* 24 days
Weight (F)	442–700g	**Fledging**	?

Identification The male Falcated Teal is one of the most beautiful of the *Anas* ducks and at first sight appears much more likely to be related to the Mandarin and Wood Duck (*Aix* spp.). The dark head is boldly patterned in iridescent purple and green with a white throat and black collar and extended drooping crest. The body is delicately patterned in grey, and the highly extended black and white secondaries arch over the black and yellow rear quarters to produce an unmistakable combination of shape and colour. The female is rather like other surface-feeding ducks, with mottled brown and buff plumage, but like the male she has a crest which imparts a slightly large-headed appearance.

Adult female

Adult female

Habitat Breeds by water meadows and lakes in both open and lightly wooded country. Winters mainly on flood meadows but is also found on rivers, coastal lagoons and estuaries.
Nest Usually close to water, amongst marshy tussocks or under cover of low bushes.
Food Mainly vegetarian, feeding on aquatic plants by dabbling and up-ending, and grazing waterside vegetation.
Range Known breeding range covers far eastern Siberia and Japan. Nesting records exist as far west as the Yenesei River and as far east as Kamchatka but the region is remote and detailed information is not available.
Movements Falcated Teal are highly migratory, wintering from Japan and Korea south through much of China to central Vietnam and westward in small numbers to northeast India.

RECORD OF SIGHTINGS	
Date ______	Date ______
Place ______	Place ______
Male(s) ______ Female(s) ______	Male(s) ______ Female(s) ______
Immature ______ Eclipse ______	Immature ______ Eclipse ______
Behaviour Notes	

Baikal Teal

Anas formosa 34 – 36cm **MAP 49**

Wing (M)	200 – 220mm	**Egg colour**	Green-grey
Wing (F)	180 – 210mm	**Clutch size**	6 – 9
Weight (M)	500 – 600g	**Incubation**	?
Weight (F)	500 – 600g	**Fledging**	?

Identification When fresh, the feathers on the drake Baikal Teal's head are tipped with buff which softens their colours, but the tips are quickly worn away to reveal a stunning plumage of green and gold, separated by swirling lines of black and white. The breast is warm buff with dark markings, the flanks are grey, and long black, yellow and buff plumes cascade over the back. The female Baikal is very like other *Anas* ducks except for a slightly darker and more distinct spotting on the plumage, but is easily identified by the unique face pattern. Dark lines run through the eye both horizontally and vertically to form a cross.

Habitat Breeds by pools in the northern forests (taiga) and on

Subdued colours of male in fresh plumage.

Male in eclipse looks very like the female.

marshes and river deltas at the edge of the tundra. Winters in both freshwater and brackish lowland habitats.

Nest A grassy hollow on the ground, usually under cover of shrubby vegetation close to water. A lining of down is added once incubation has begun.

Food Vegetarian. The birds feed mainly by dabbling, but also feed among growing crops and in stubble fields.

Range The breeding range covers a broad sweep across northeast Siberia from the Angara River east to Kamchatka and from the Arctic coast south to Lake Baikal.

Movements At the end of the short breeding season the birds fly south to winter in Japan, southeastern China and Formosa.

RECORD OF SIGHTINGS	
Date ______	Date ______
Place ______	Place ______
Male(s) ______ Female(s) ______	Male(s) ______ Female(s) ______
Immature ______ Eclipse ______	Immature ______ Eclipse ______
Behaviour Notes	

Spotbill Duck

Anas poecilorhyncha 58–63cm **MAP 50**

Wing (M)	256–293mm	**Egg colour**	Grey-buff
Wing (F)	240–265mm	**Clutch size**	6–12
Weight (M)	1230–1500g	**Incubation**	*c* 24 days
Weight (F)	790–1360g	**Fledging**	?

Identification The Chinese Spotbill *A. p. zonorhyncha* (illustrated) is the most northerly of three distinct subspecies. The others are the Indian and the Burmese. The Chinese Spotbill is considerably darker than the southern races and differs from them in having no white bar along the rear edge of the speculum. Also, the speculum itself is deep blue in this species; green in the others. Both male and female resemble chunky, but greyer, female Mallard in their dappled brown and buff plumage and distinctive dark cap and eye-stripe. The bill is black with a brilliant yellow tip, and in the southern races there are two orange-red spots at the base of the bill, from which the species gets its name.

Above: The much paler, greyer, Indian Spotbill (AA.p.poecilorhyncha) showing the characteristic red spots at the base of the bill. **Below:** Adult Chinese Spotbill.

Habitat Shallow freshwater lakes and marshes; also rice fields.
Nest A platform constructed of aquatic vegetation, in the marsh or in cover on the lake bank close to the water.
Food Vegetarian. Feeds by dabbling and up-ending and also by wading among emergent growth in shallows. Spotbills feed morning and evening, often in small flocks or family groups.
Range Southern races inhabit India and Bangladesh eastward across Burma, Thailand, Laos and Vietnam. The Chinese Spotbill extends across much of southern and eastern China, adjacent parts of Siberia, Korea and the Japanese islands.
Movements Northernmost breeding populations migrate to south and east China in winter. Over much of the southern range the species is a year-round resident.

RECORD OF SIGHTINGS	
Date ________	Date ________
Place ________	Place ________
Male(s) ____ Female(s) ____	Male(s) ____ Female(s) ____
Immature ____ Eclipse ____	Immature ____ Eclipse ____
Behaviour Notes	

Baer's Pochard

Aythya baeri 41–46cm **MAP 51**

Wing (M)	210–233mm	**Egg colour**	Yellow-grey
Wing (F)	186–203mm	**Clutch size**	*c* 10
Weight (M)	?	**Incubation**	?
Weight (F)	?	**Fledging**	?

Identification When seen on the water, Baer's Pochard is very like the Ferruginous Duck, in whose company it may be seen in east Asia in winter or on migration. The drake has a black head with a metallic green sheen, the upperparts are dark brown, the breast and flanks a rich chestnut with a white patch at the rear end, and the belly white. The female is similar but lacks the metallic sheen on the head and has a chestnut patch on the face at the base of the bill. In both sexes the bill is large and blue-grey in colour. A useful identifying feature is the rounded head, which lacks the prominent high crown of the Ferruginous Duck.

Habitat In summer the bird inhabits open areas dotted with lakes

with abundant emergent vegetation. Winter is spent on more open freshwater lakes, slow rivers and marshes.

Nest Little detail is known but the bird probably nests on the ground among lakeside vegetation.

Food Details of diet are not known, but the birds are thought to feed almost entirely by diving.

Range The breeding range is restricted to the eastern USSR near the mouths of the Ussuri and Amur rivers, on the Khanka plain and among the lakes of the Poset region.

Movements The main wintering areas are in China around the Gulf of Chihli, south to the Yangtze, and in Fukien. There are winter populations also in Assam, Bangladesh and Burma, and less commonly in Japan and Korea.

RECORD OF SIGHTINGS	
Date ______	Date ______
Place ______	Place ______
Male(s) ______ Female(s) ______	Male(s) ______ Female(s) ______
Immature ______ Eclipse ______	Immature ______ Eclipse ______
Behaviour Notes	

Chinese Merganser

Mergus squamatus 52–62cm **MAP 52**

Wing (M)	250–265mm	**Egg colour**	?
Wing (F)	240–250mm	**Clutch size**	?
Weight (M)	?	**Incubation**	?
Weight (F)	?	**Fledging**	?

Identification The Chinese Merganser is one of the rarest and least-known members of the sawbill family. It is closely related to the Red-breasted Merganser, and both male and female bear a close resemblance to that species. The drake has a glossy black head and neck shot with green, and a long wispy crest. It is best distinguished from the Red-breasted Merganser by its plain white breast and by the scale-like pattern of black markings along its flanks (from which it gets its alternative name of Scaly or Scaly-sided Merganser). The female has a warm buff head, pale grey back, and a lighter pattern of scale markings on the flanks.

Habitat The birds breed by small fast-flowing rivers in forested hill country, and winter on more open lakes and larger rivers. There is some movement downstream but the birds do not winter in coastal habitats.
Nest The eggs are laid in holes in old or damaged trees, close to or overhanging the river.
Food Probably mainly fish, caught by diving in the fast-flowing waters and swirling pools. Details not known.
Range The species is resident in the southeastern USSR and northeastern Manchuria, notably along the Amur River.
Movements Apart from local downstream movements in winter the species is not migratory. There are irregular winter dispersals, possibly due to severe weather, in which birds have been recorded as far south as North Vietnam.

RECORD OF SIGHTINGS	
Date ______	Date ______
Place ______	Place ______
Male(s) ______ Female(s) ______	Male(s) ______ Female(s) ______
Immature ______ Eclipse ______	Immature ______ Eclipse ______
Behaviour Notes	

Map Section

The maps that follow show the geographical distribution of the 52 Northern Hemisphere duck species. Principal breeding areas are shown in red; wintering areas are shown in blue.

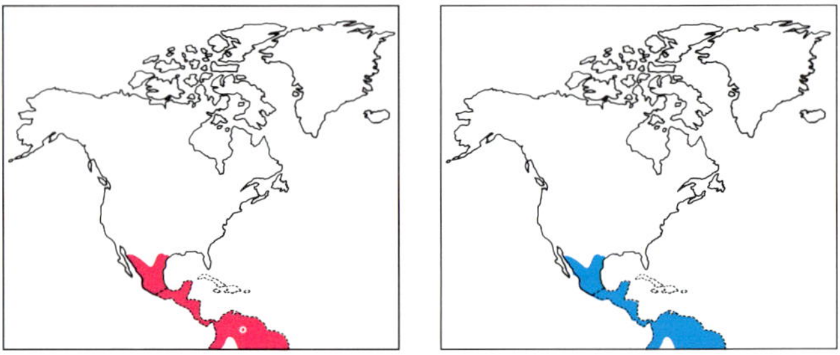

MAP 1 Black-bellied Whistling Duck *Dendrocygna autumnalis*

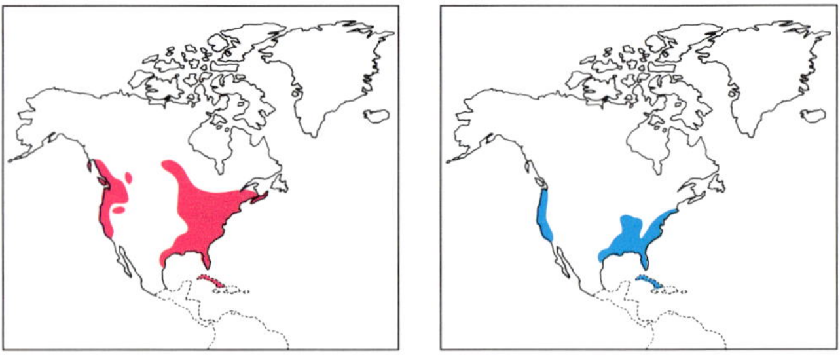

MAP 2 Wood Duck *Aix sponsa*

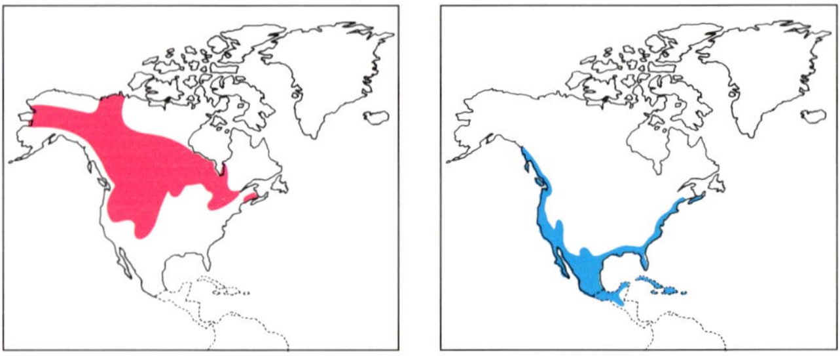

MAP 3 American Wigeon *Anas americana*

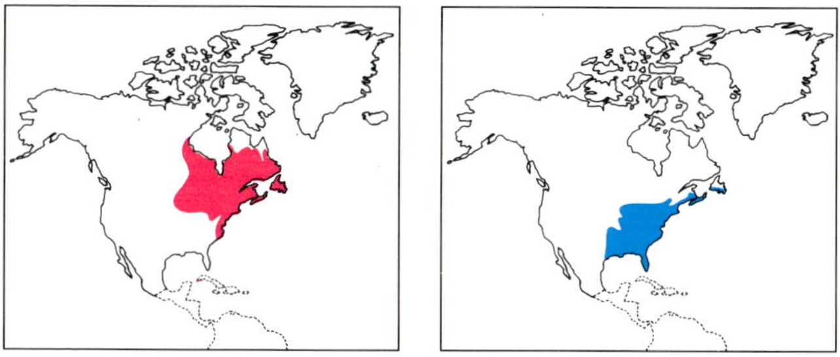

MAP 4 Black Duck *Anas rubripes*

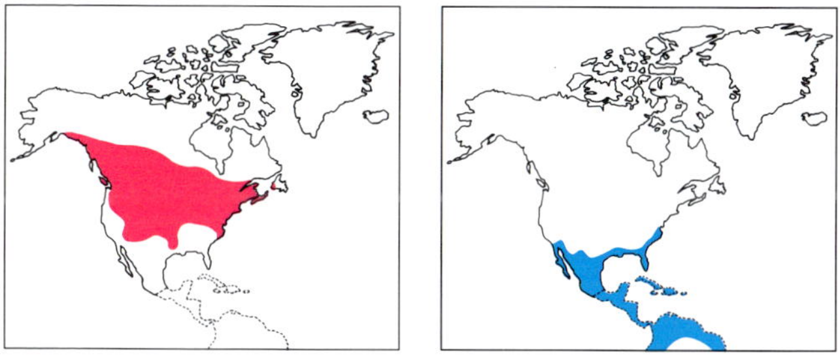

MAP 5 Blue-winged Teal *Anas discors*

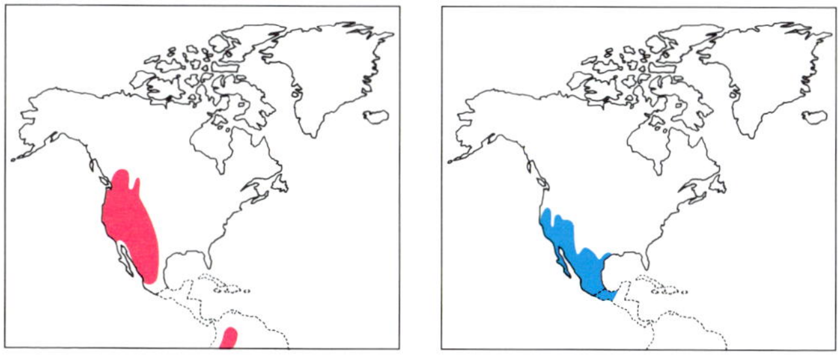

MAP 6 Cinnamon Teal *Anas cyanoptera*

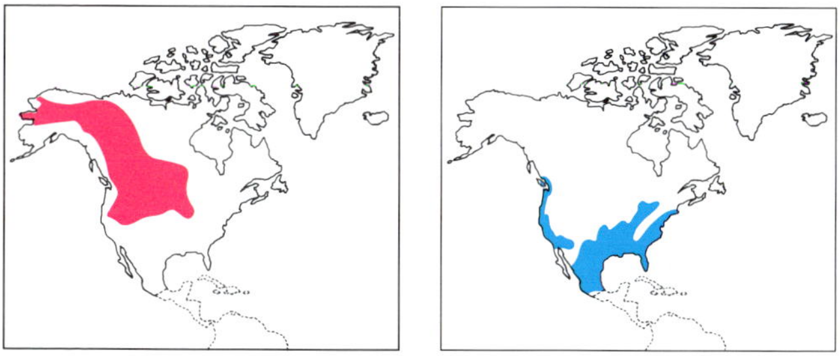

MAP 7 Canvasback *Aythya valisineria*

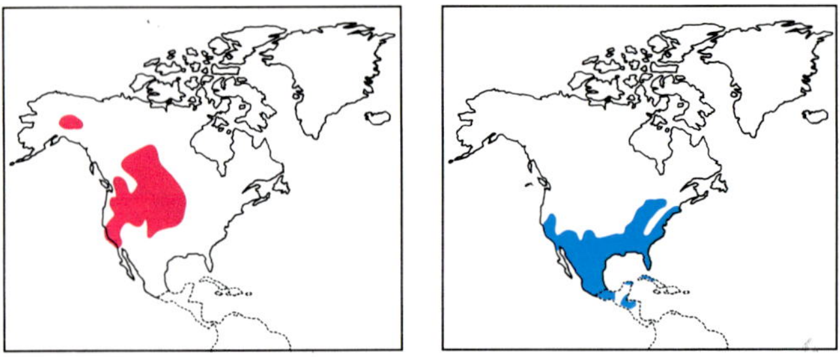

MAP 8 Redhead *Aythya americana*

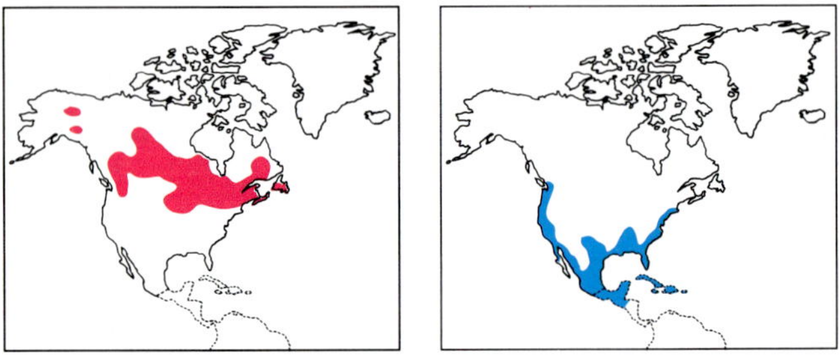

MAP 9 Ring-necked Duck *Aythya collaris*

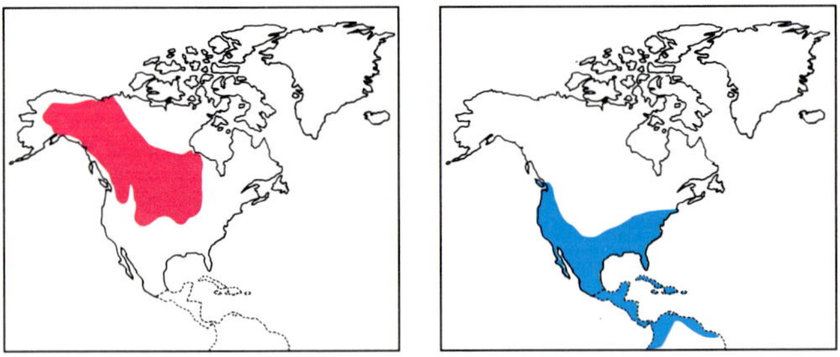

MAP 10 Lesser Scaup *Aythya affinis*

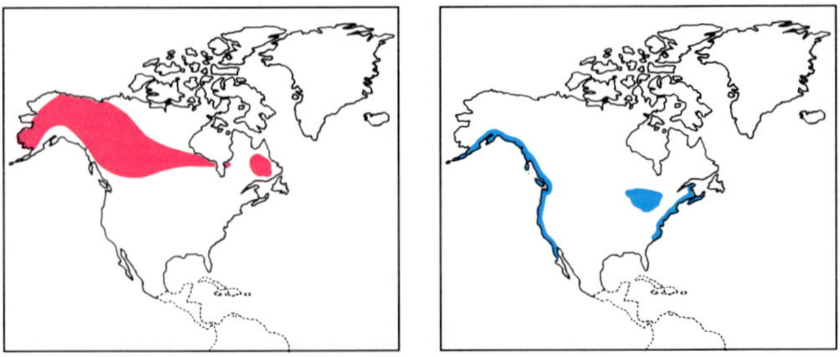

MAP 11 Surf Scoter *Melanitta perspicillata*

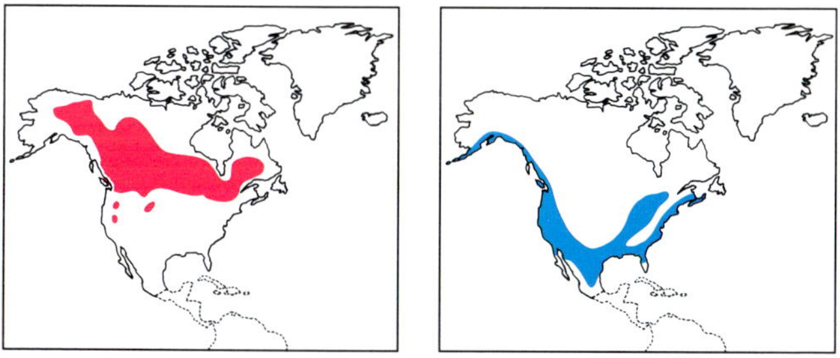

MAP 12 Bufflehead *Bucephala albeola*

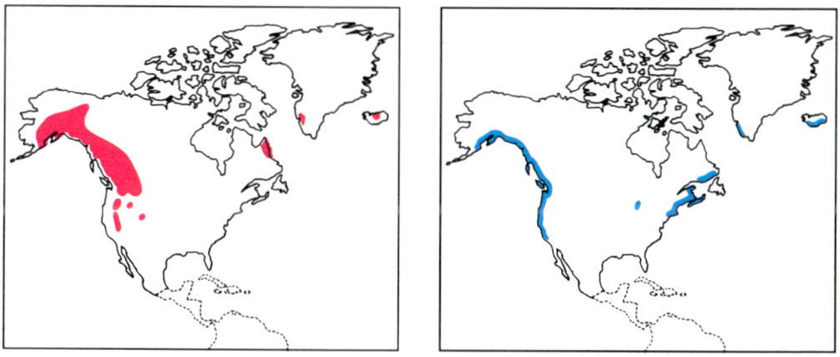

MAP 13 Barrow's Goldeneye *Bucephala islandica*

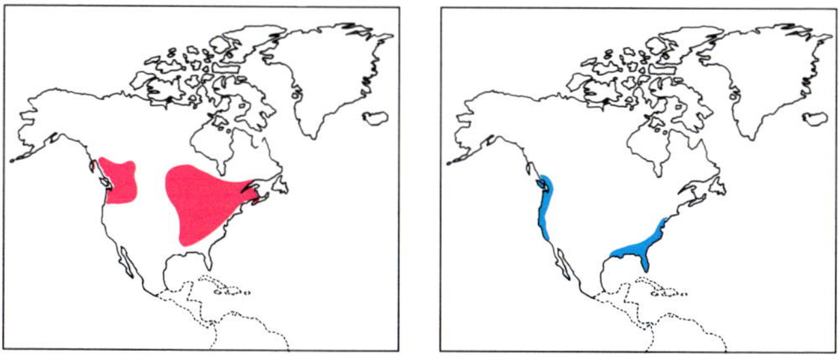

MAP 14 Hooded Merganser *Mergus cucullatus*

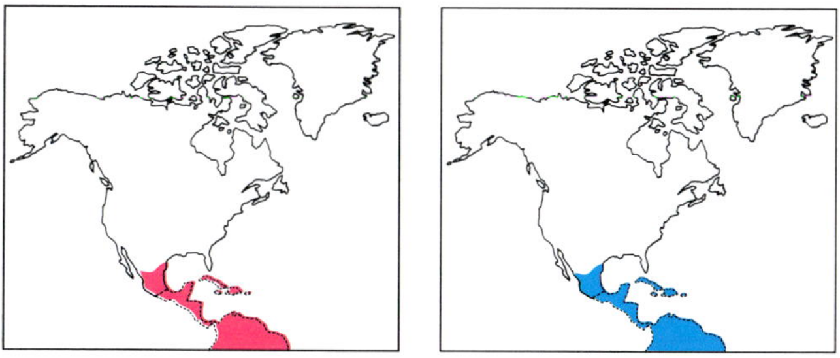

MAP 15 Masked Duck *Oxyura dominica*

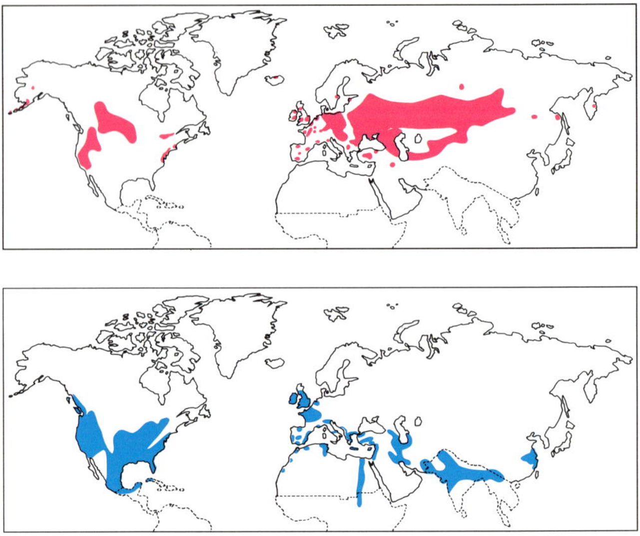

MAP 16 Gadwall *Anas strepera*

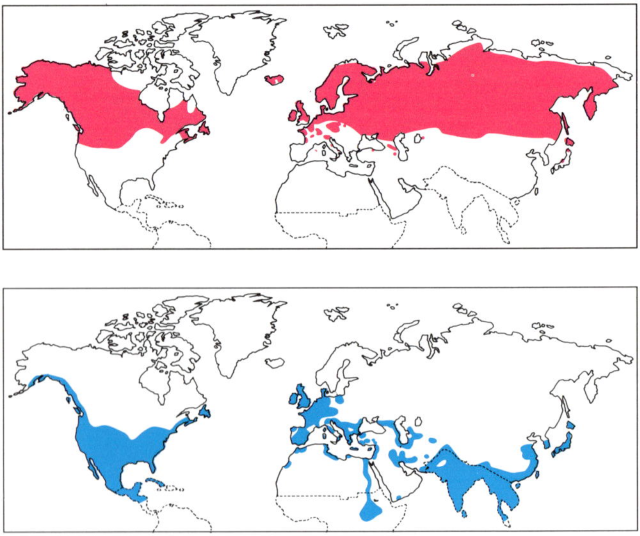

MAP 17 Green-winged Teal *Anas crecca*

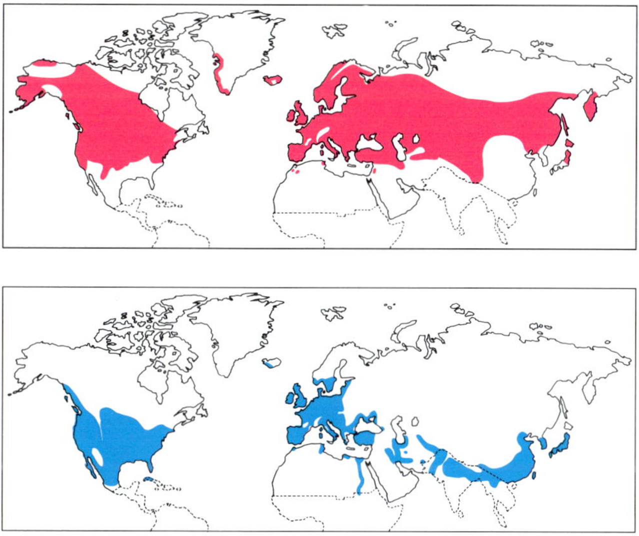

MAP 18 Mallard *Anas platyrhynchos*

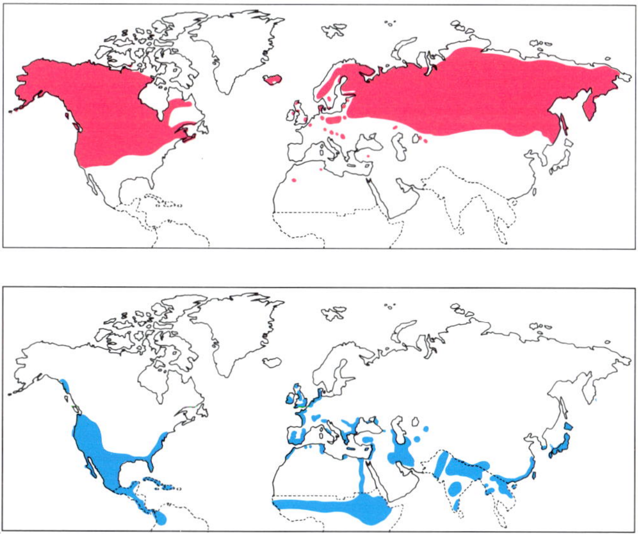

MAP 19 Pintail *Anas acuta*

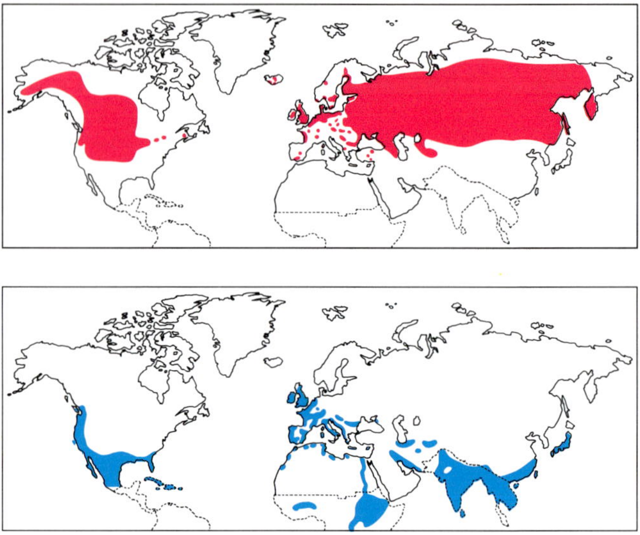

MAP 20 Northern Shoveler *Anas clypeata*

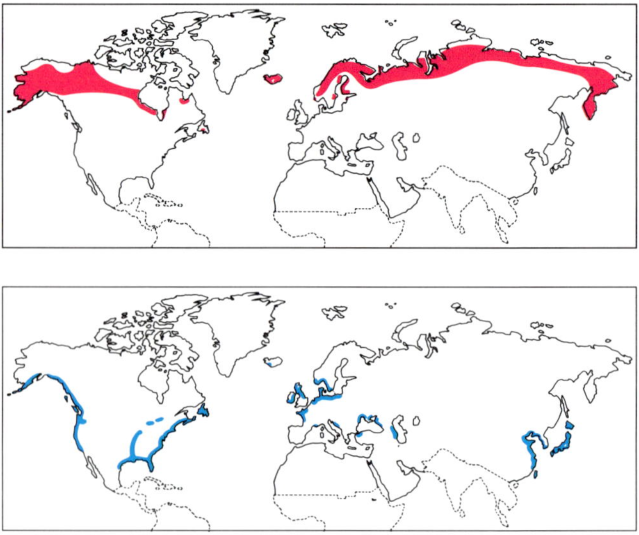

MAP 21 Greater Scaup *Aythya marila*

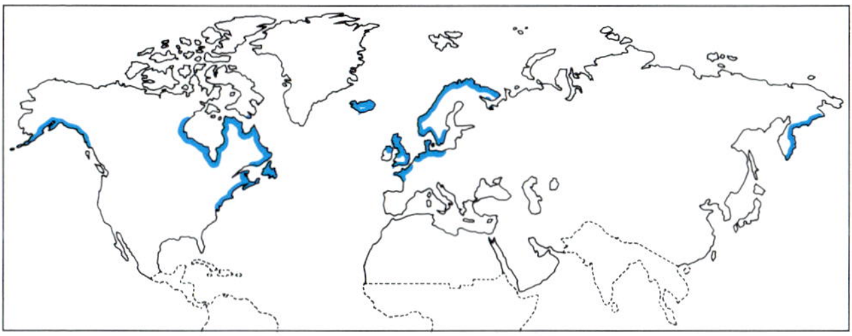

MAP 22 Common Eider *Somateria mollissima*

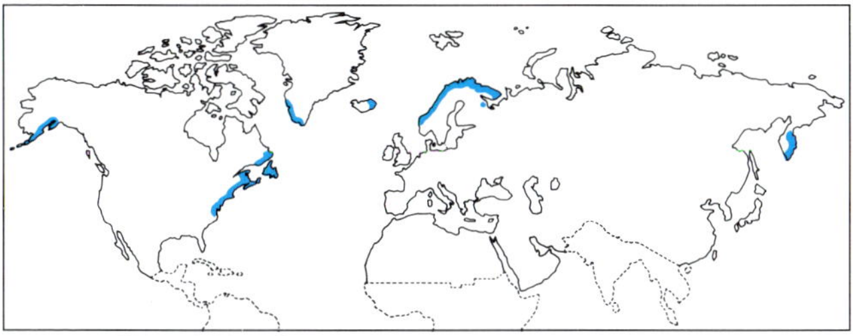

MAP 23 King Eider *Somateria spectabilis*

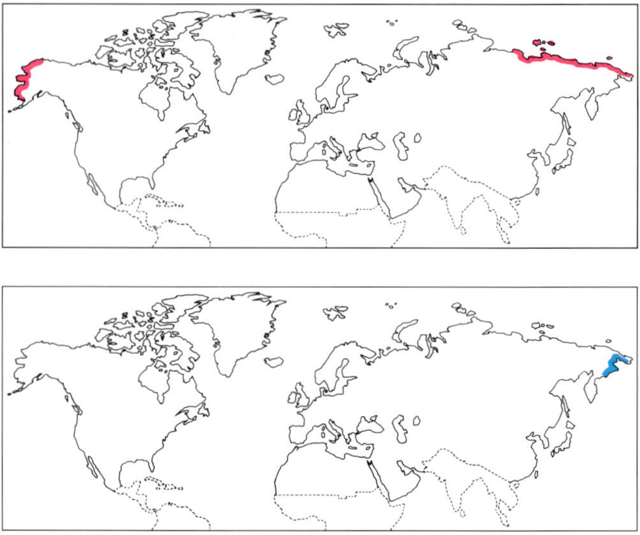

MAP 24 Spectacled Eider *Somateria fischeri*

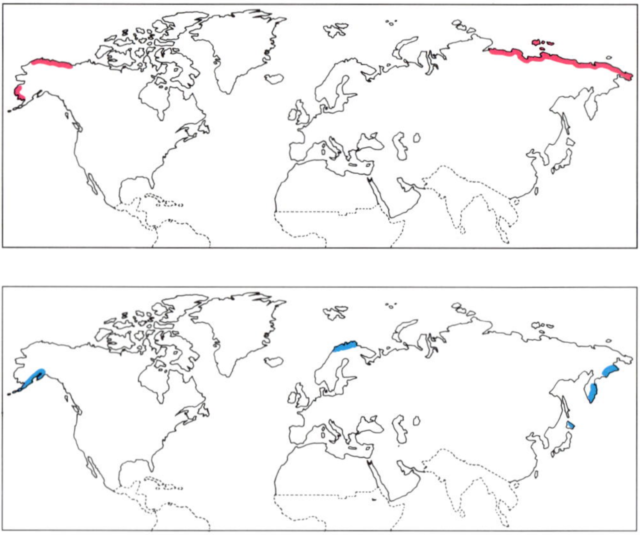

MAP 25 Steller's Eider *Polysticta stelleri*

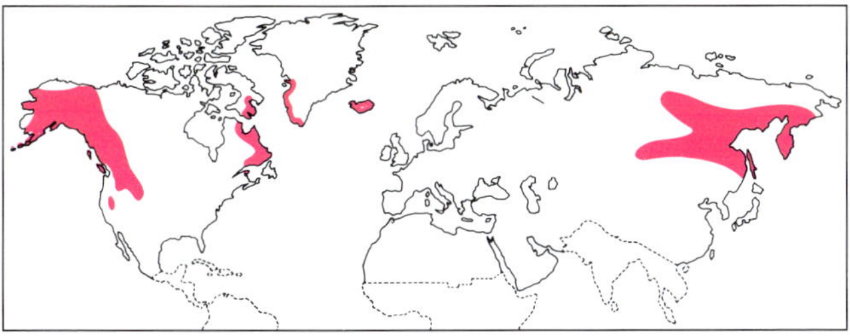

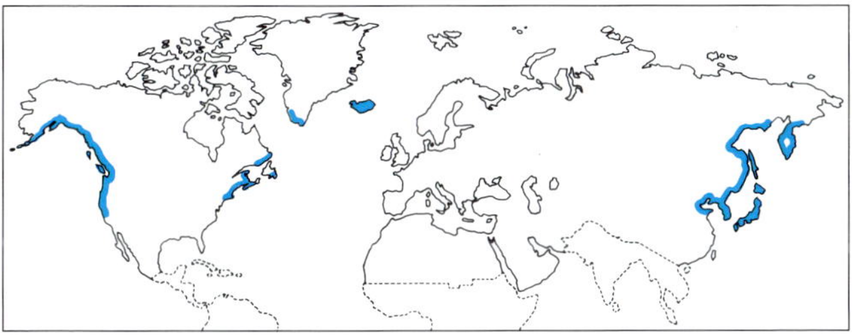

MAP 26 Harlequin Duck *Histrionicus histrionicus*

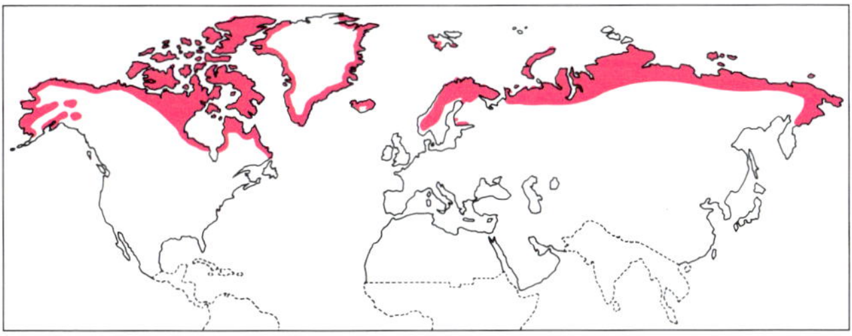

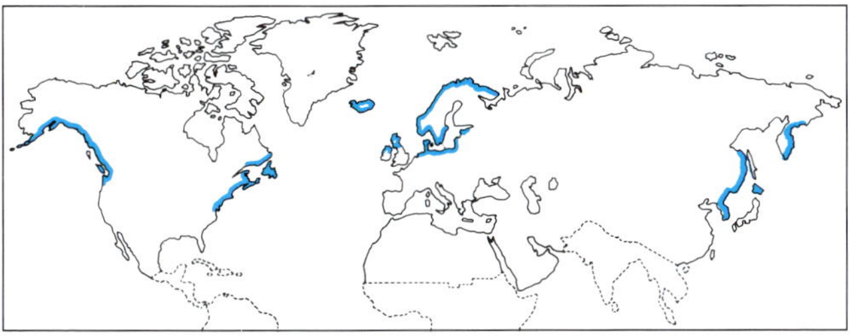

MAP 27 Old squaw *Clangula hyemalis*

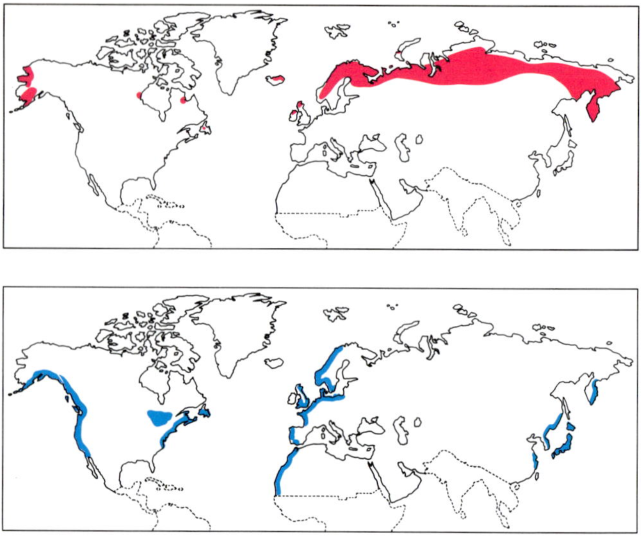

MAP 28 Common Scoter *Melanitta nigra*

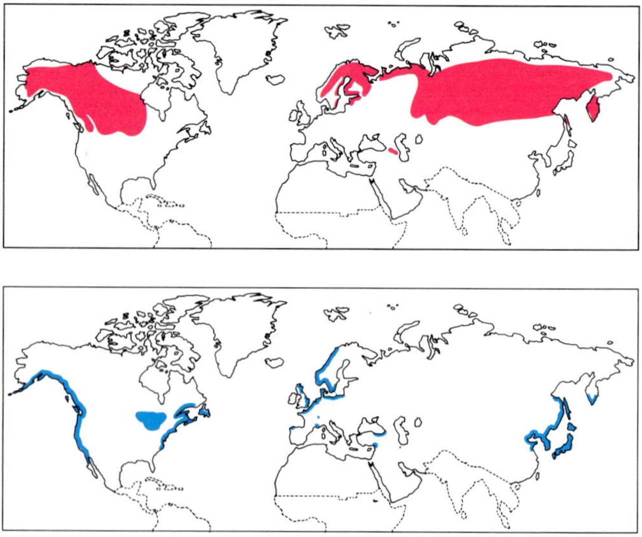

MAP 29 Velvet Scoter *Melanitta fusca*

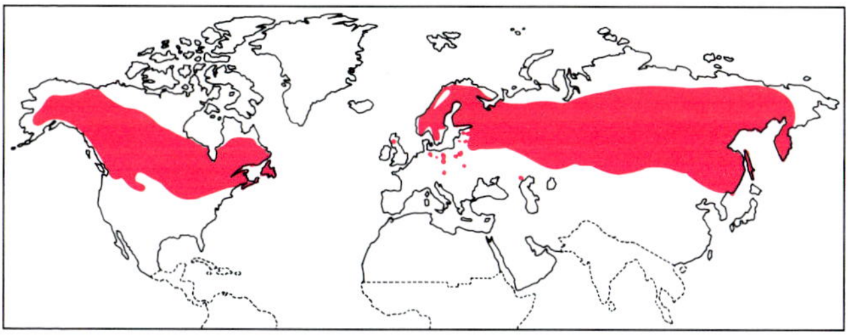

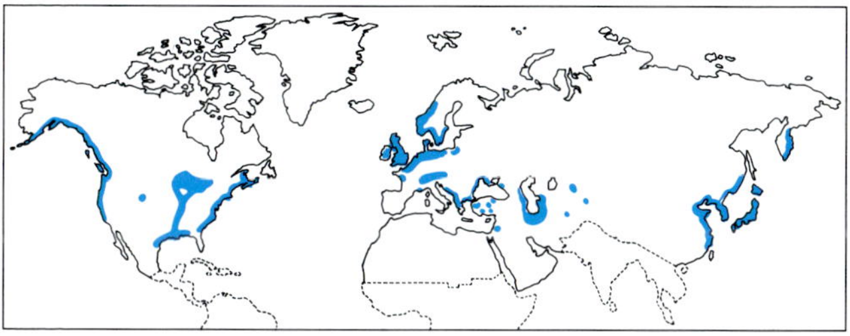

MAP 30 Common Goldeneye *Bucephala clangula*

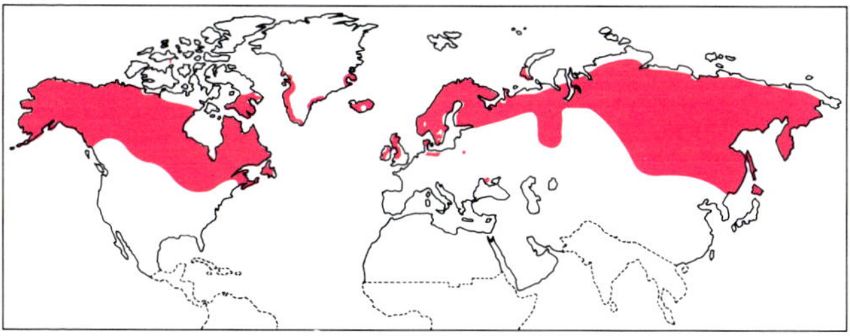

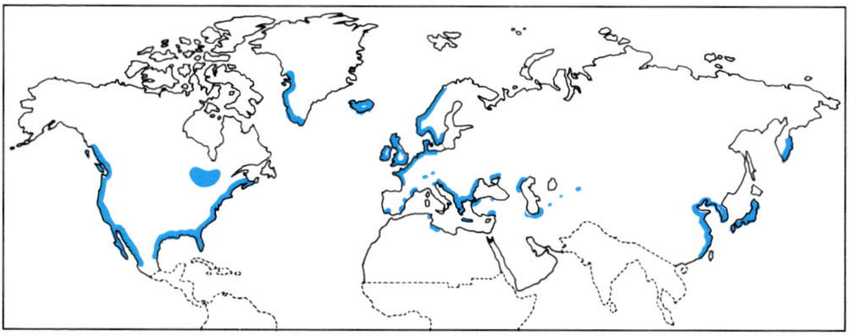

MAP 31 Red-breasted Merganser *Mergus serrator*

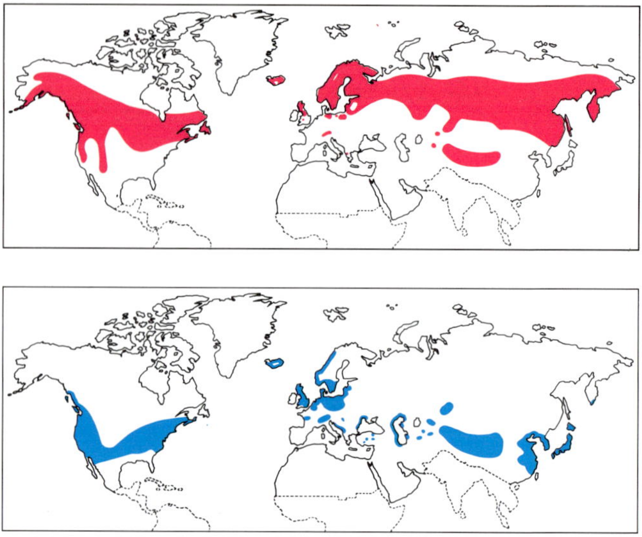

MAP 32 Common Merganser *Mergus merganser*

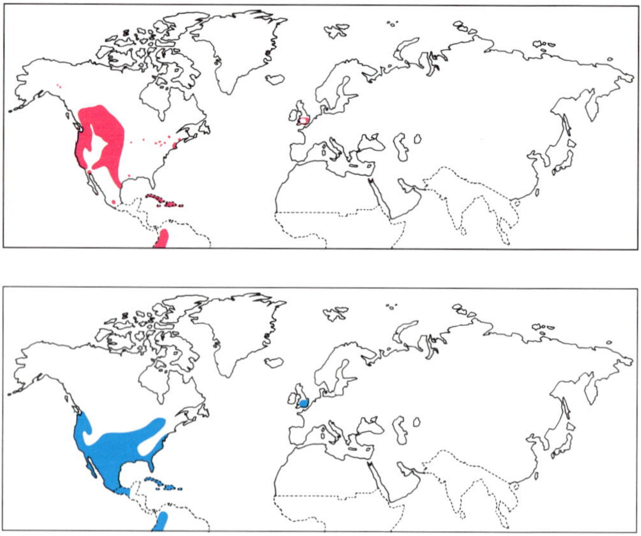

MAP 33 Ruddy Duck *Oxyura jamaicensis*

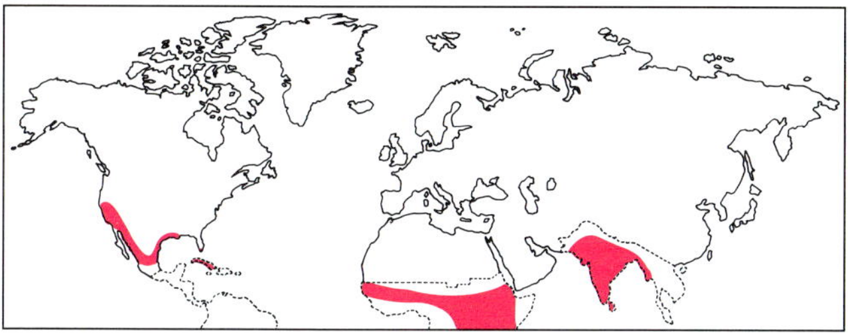

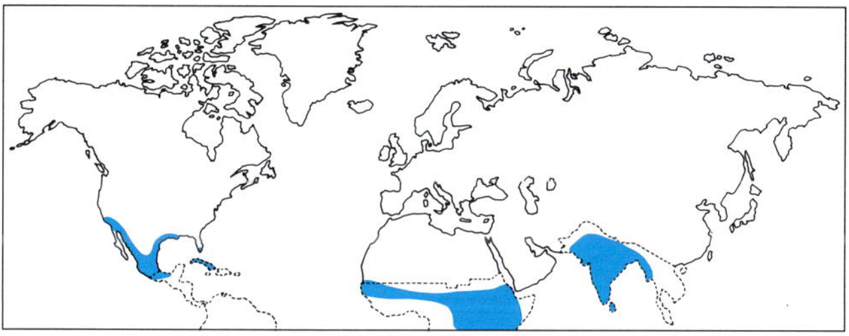

MAP 34 Fulvous Whistling Duck *Dendrocygna bicolor*

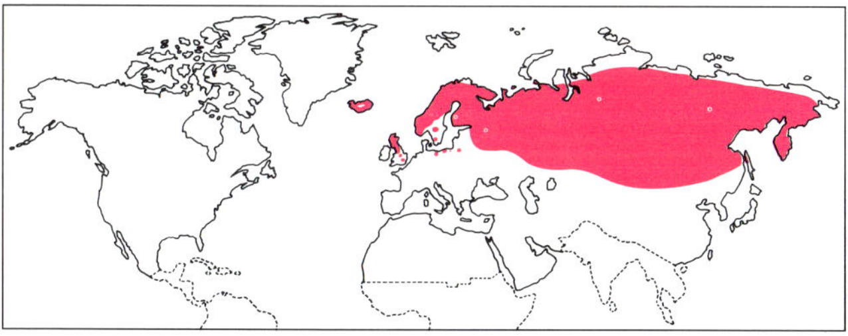

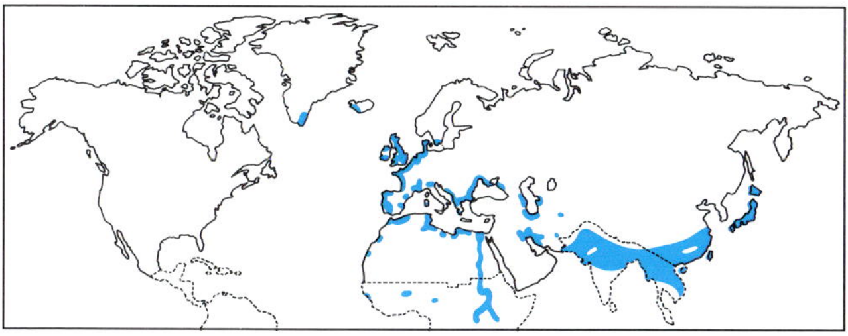

MAP 35 European Wigeon *Anas penelope*

MAP 36
Egyptian Goose
Alopochen aegyptiacus

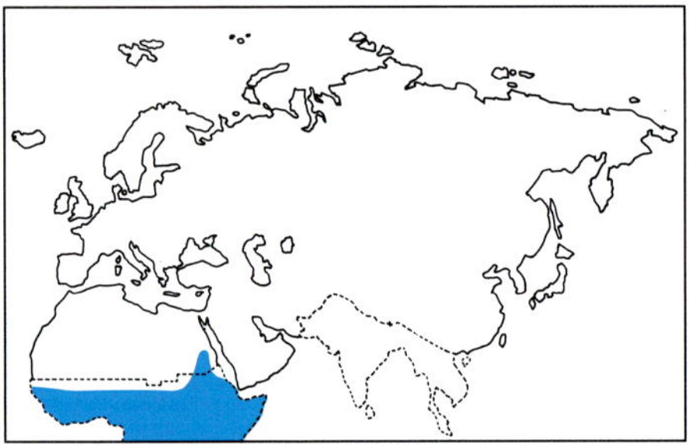

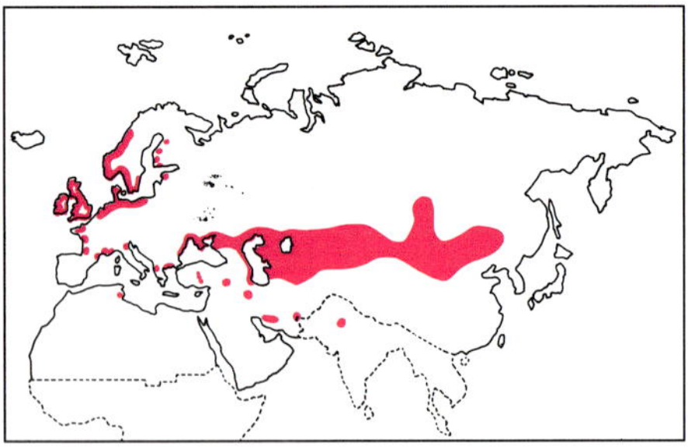

MAP 37
Shelduck
Tadorna tadorna

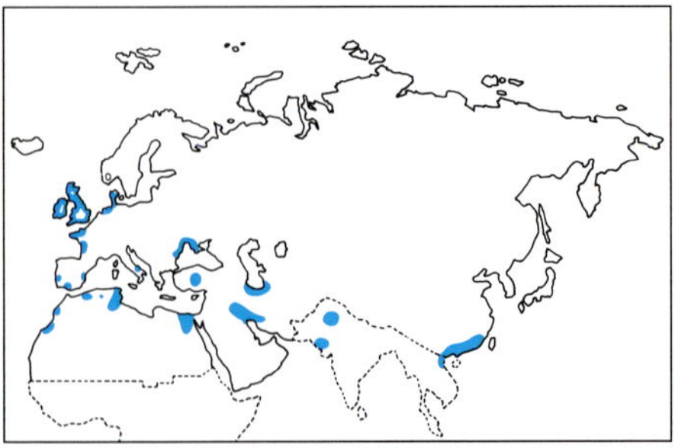

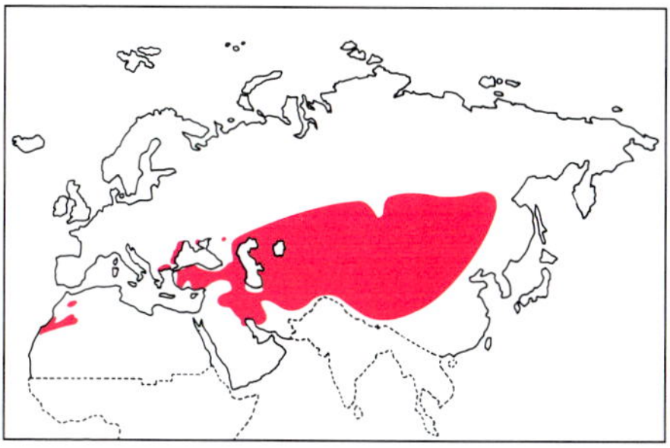

MAP 38
Ruddy Shelduck
Tadorna ferruginea

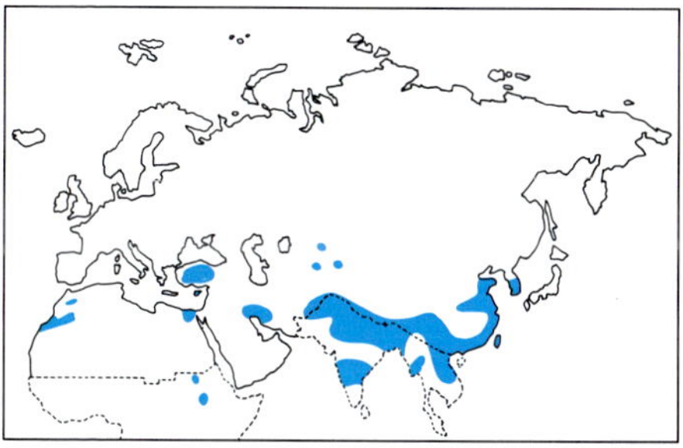

MAP 39
Mandarin Duck
Aix galericulata

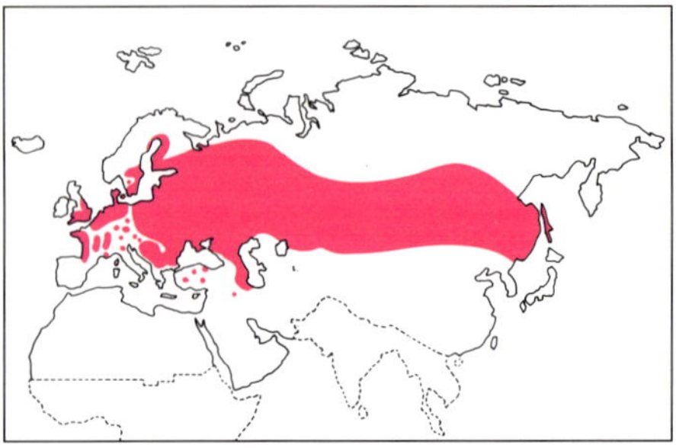

MAP 40
Garganey
Anas querquedula

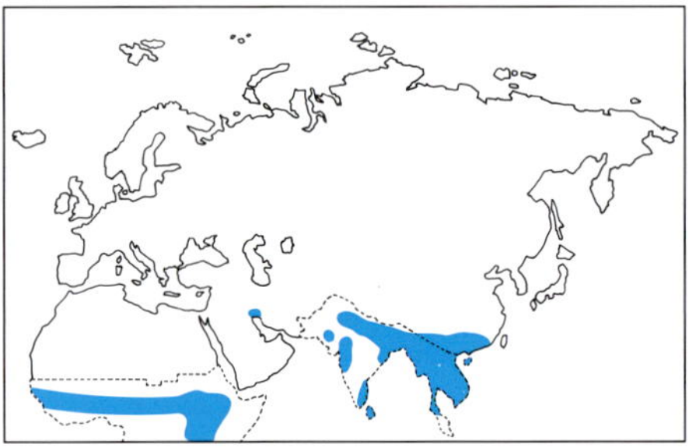

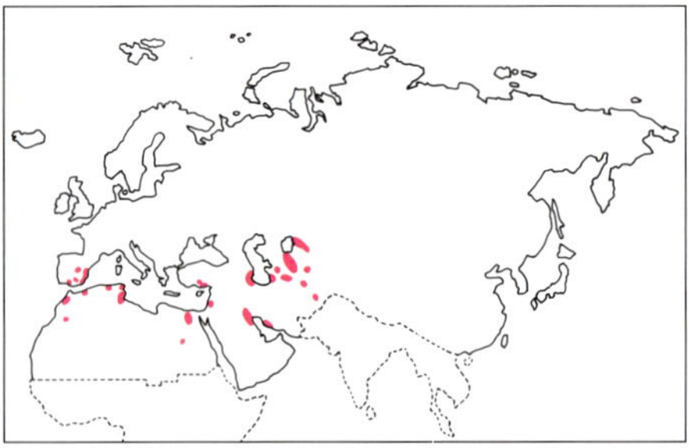

MAP 41
Marbled Teal
Marmaronetta angustirostris

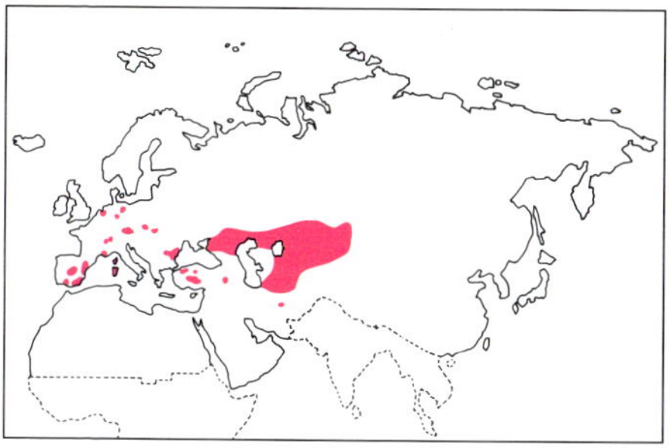

MAP 42
Red-crested Pochard
Netta rufina

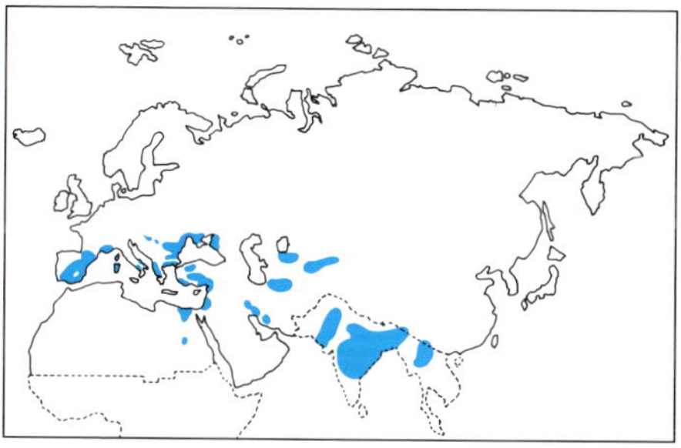

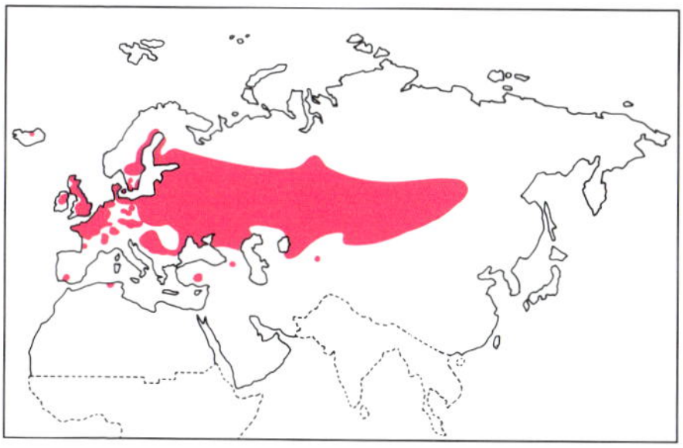

MAP 43
Pochard
Aythya ferina

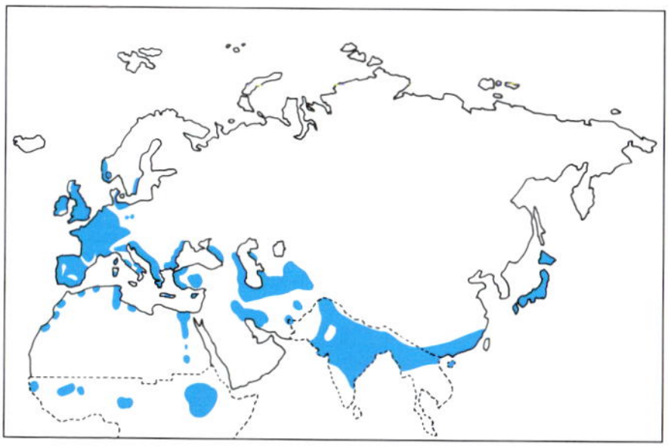

MAP 44
Ferruginous Duck
Aythya nyroca

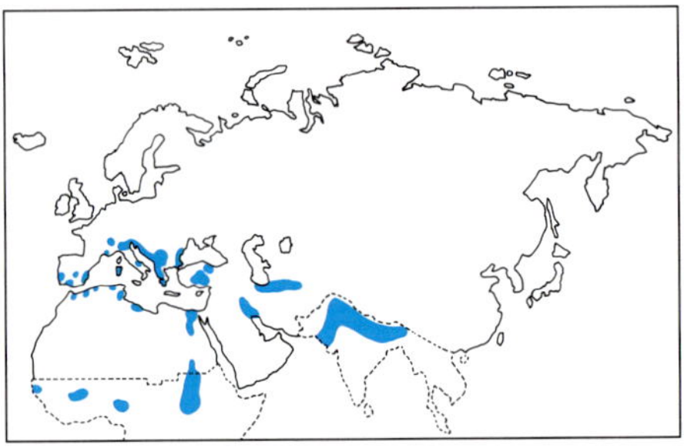

MAP 45
Tufted Duck
Aythya fuligula

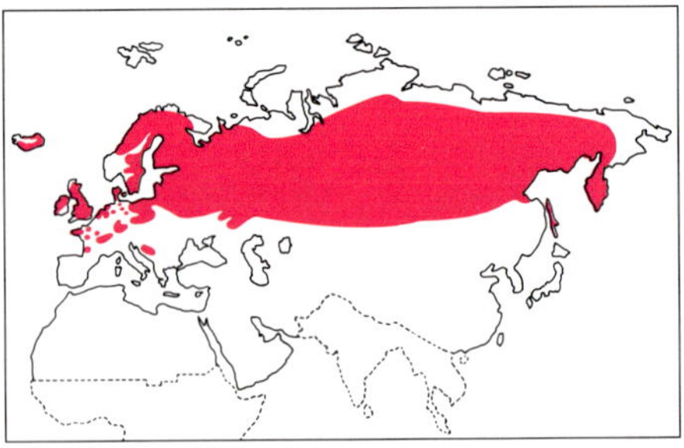

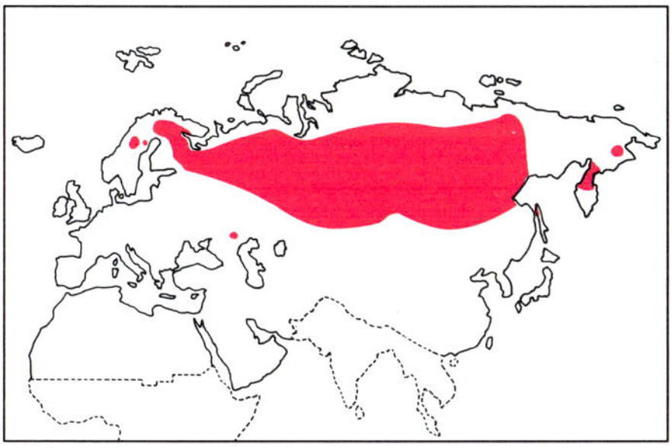

MAP 46
Smew
Mergus albellus

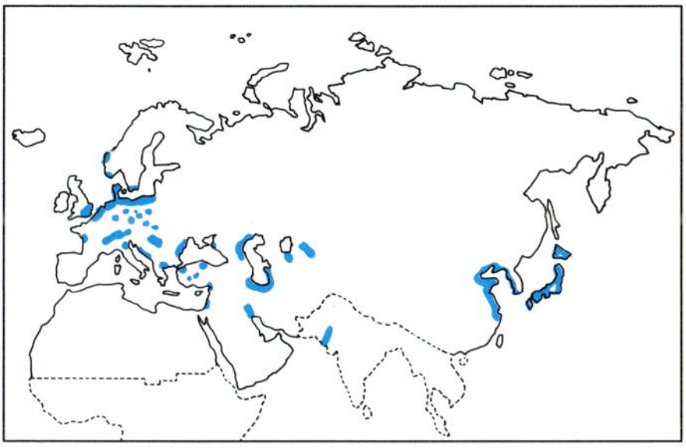

MAP 47
White-headed Duck
Oxyura leucocephala

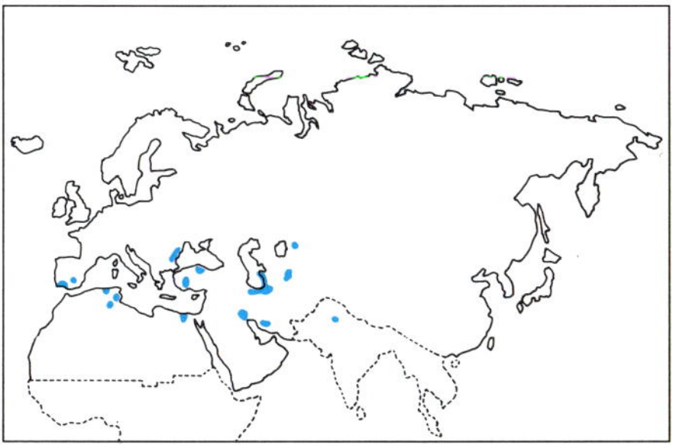

MAP 48
Falcated Teal
Anas falcata

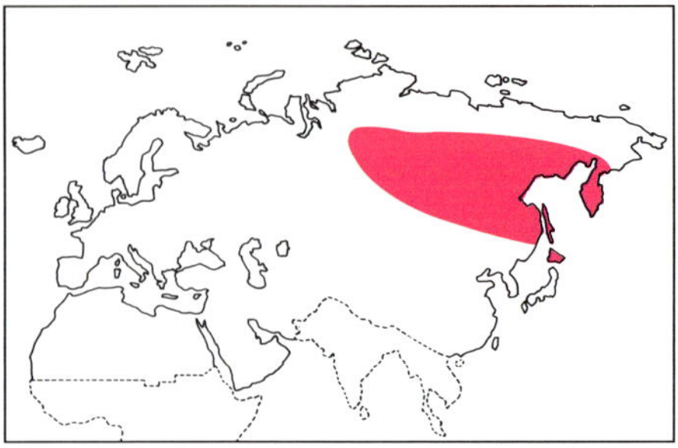

MAP 49
Baikal Teal
Anas formosa

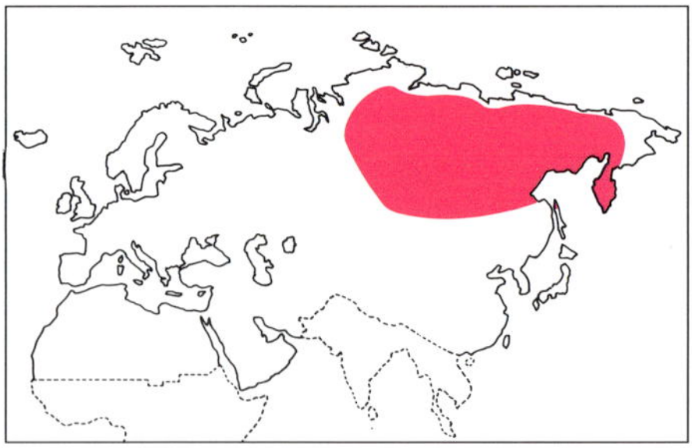

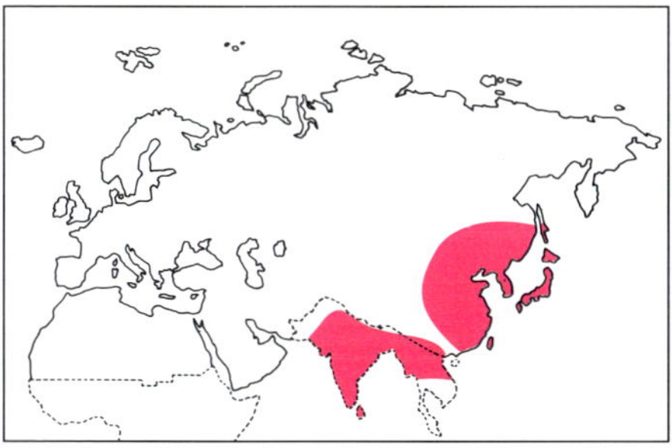

MAP 50
Spotbill Duck
Anas poecilorhyncha

MAP 51
Baer's Pochard
Aythya baeri

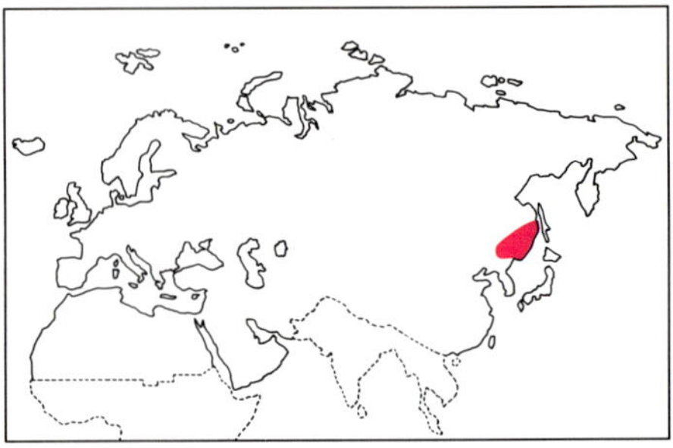

MAP 52
Chinese Merganser
Mergus squamatus

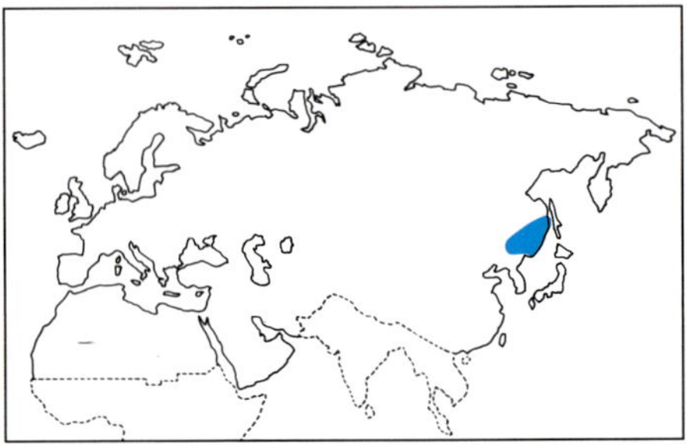

Index

RSNC

The Royal Society for Nature Conservation is pleased to endorse these excellent, fully illustrated pocket guide books which provide invaluable information on the wildlife of Britain and Northern Europe. Royalties from each book sold will go to help the RSNC's network of 48 Wildlife Trusts and over 50 Urban Wildlife Groups, all working to protect rare and endangered wildlife and threatened habitats. The RSNC and the Wildlife Trusts have a combined membership of 184,000 and look after over 1,800 nature reserves. If you would like to find out more, please contact the RSNC, The Green, Nettleham, Lincoln, LN2 2NR, Telephone 0522 752326.